2020

Daughter ot the Depression

My Life Remembered

Mary Philips

Edited by Rebecca Bolin

Cover Design by Lacey Brewer

DEDICATION

*In loving memory of Reverend Robert Thompson,
the most influential man in my life.*

Our Pastor
(composed when I was in high school)

I'll never forget him whatever be the tide,
And in him always friendship will abide.
He looks about him with never a frown,
but with a smile so dear.
When things seem to go from bad to worse,
he brings hope and cheer.

He looks at the stars; wonder in his eyes
that trouble can never erase.
He talks earnestly and hopefully to God,
love shining in his serene face.

When you hear his message so lovely expressed
God seems to be so near.
He seems to talk straight to God
It drives away your fear.

To everyone he is a friend;
his hand has strength and power.
To him I'll ask a safe return,
as I commune with God in prayer.

CONTENTS

ACKNOWLEDGMENTS

I wish to thank Lacey for doing such an outstanding job on the cover design. Thank you to all my children, grandchildren, and great-grandchildren for your encouragement, love, and support over the years. I also want to thank my teachers and mentors who encouraged me to write. Finally, I want to thank my Heavenly Father who has preserved me for such a time as this.

Introduction
by Rebecca Bolin

It is has been my mother's lifelong dream to see her work in print for audiences around the world. In 2017, I conducted several hours of interviews with her over the course of eight months. I digitally recorded her stories and memories and carefully transcribed them in order to obtain a written record. I created a *Family History* from those interviews and shared it with family members, but my mother, Mary Ruth Philips, could not let go of the idea that her work should be published. She would often ask me about it, and without pressuring me, would let me know that she was not letting her dream die. Once in a card to me she wrote, "I'm looking forward to seeing the book, Rebecca. But take your time. I know you have lots to do." And so with due diligence, and careful attention to the accuracy and spirit of her words, I have compiled her story here. I characterize this work as an autobiography, as it is told in her own words and combines real-life events with historical information.

This is the story of a young woman who grew up during one of the bleakest moments in our country's history. Like many around her, she lived in the shadow of poverty, yet nurtured private goals, dreams, and aspirations. She faced hardships and deprivation with an unwavering faith in God. She asked for little and was content with the meanest existence as long, as she had her children around her and a relationship with her loving Heavenly Father. She spent her life caring for others and putting their needs ahead of her own, and only now, at the age of eighty-eight, is she finally seeing her dreams fulfilled.

THE EARLY YEARS

I was born at the worst possible time for my parents. They were married on Christmas Eve, in the year of our Lord, 1930. My mother, Ruth Lavandie Whirley, was a homemaker, and my father, Charlie Abner Cason, was a sharecropper. They were both twenty-three years old when they said, "I do" at a little church in Fannin County, Texas. With very few possessions, their love for each other, and their dreams of a bright future, they moved into a little one-room house known as Lowry's Place in Windom, Texas. Nine months and seven days later, I was born, right in the middle of what became known as The Great Depression.

The stock market had crashed in 1929, and many people believed Texas would be protected from economic crisis, because its rural economy was primarily driven by the agricultural industry in the north and oil in the west. Then, in the latter half of 1930, the Dust Bowl hit, devastating the Panhandle and the southern plains and making life on farms and in many towns next to impossible. Fannin County is located in Northeast Texas and shares a border with Oklahoma. The agricultural industry was the primary source of income for local residents with cotton and corn crops leading the way. During the Depression, close to ten thousand people, mostly farmers, left Fannin County, seeking a better life elsewhere.[1]

My parents quickly realized that their sporadic farming wages would not be enough to pay rent, put food on the table, and care for a child, so with me in tow, they sheepishly moved back in with my dad's parents, Eliza Deborah and John Abner Cason on the Mrs. Jenny Reed Farm in Windom. I called my grandfather, Pappa [**pæ**-pä] Cason, and my grandmother, Mamma [**mæ**-mä] Cason. Pappa Cason was very attached to me, and he nicknamed me Nooks. When I was very little, I would crawl across the porch, and he would walk along beside me and hold on to the tail of my dress to keep me from falling off. When I would nearly get to the end of the porch, he would say, "Wait a minute, Nooks! Don't fall!" I don't quite remember him, but my parents told me that story many times, and when I think about Pappa Cason, something stirs within my emotions, and I feel close to him in my heart.

Although my memories of my paternal grandfather are vague, I definitely remember Mamma Cason. She spent quite a bit of time with me and was often my caregiver and playmate when my mother worked in the fields with my dad. She had high expectations for me, but she also knew how to make our time together entertaining, but more on her later.

While my parents and I lived on the Mrs. Jenny Reed Farm, my dad's brother and sister, John Jr. and Sallie Rhoda, still lived at home as well; the groans of the house matched the dismay of my grandparents at having so many mouths to feed. Although we were crowded, and the sources of stress were many, everyone generally kept a good attitude and helped each other. I think they were too tired to argue.

My parents named me Mary after the mother of Jesus, and Ruth, after my mother and Ruth in the Bible. My dad always used both names, so I became known as Mary Ruth, born on September 29, 1931. My dad often ran the two names together, so when he spoke to me, it sounded more like Mar-ruth. I know it must have been hard on everyone to have a newborn baby in the house with such close quarters. As I grew and began to talk, I called Uncle John, Uncle, and Aunt Salle became Auntie. Everyone worked and contributed to the household as they were able, but jobs were scarce. The house couldn't hold us all for long, and soon, my dad moved us into a tiny house known as the Luttoral Place. Once we were out, my grandparents relocated to Pattonville, near Paris, Texas in Lamar County. I guess my Pappa found some work there. With them further away, the chances of us moving back in with them were less likely.

When I was just eighteen months old, Pappa Cason had an attack of influenza that developed into pneumonia. He was seventy-eight years old, and his body was just not strong enough to recover. He died after several days of illness on March 7, 1933. He was very well-liked by the community and was greatly missed by the family and all who knew him.

Trips to visit family were few, but when I was about three, my parents took me to see Uncle, Auntie, and Mamma Cason. The plan was for me to spend a week with them. While all of the grown-ups were visiting, I decided to go explore the premises, and that's when I discovered Aunt Sallie's makeup. I had seen Auntie put it on before, so I had a pretty good idea what to do. No one seemed too concerned about my absence, so I played to my heart's content. I had so much fun opening each item and experimenting with the colors. When everyone was saying goodbye, I came out for the big reveal. When Auntie saw her lipstick and rouge smeared all over my face, she was startled, to say the least. She wasted no time in spanking me and giving me a lecture about respecting her things. Apparently, I smarted off to Mamma Cason, because I get a spanking from her as well for being "sassy." After being chastised by them both, I was a little less excited about staying for a week without my parents. I watched them drive away and wondered what the rest of the week would be like.

The next day, Uncle John decided to give me a haircut. I'm sure he had good intentions, but he chopped my hair up pretty badly. The more he cut, and the more he tried to fix it, the worse it got. Auntie couldn't stand it, so she wound up taking me to a local barber shop and had them give me a Buster Brown cut. Years later, Auntie and Uncle John still laughed about that haircut.

After a couple of years, my parents moved to the Chaney Place. The Chaneys had two daughters in their late teens named Edna and Lydia May. They styled hair for the public, and I loved to sit in their shop and watch them. When I got home, I would get a glass of water and a comb and sit in front of a mirror. I would wet my hair and try to make it look like theirs. Edna and Lydia May must have enjoyed having me around, because they would also give me their school papers, and I would draw pictures on the back of their work. For the first several years of my life, most of my interaction was with adults. I didn't really have any playmates, but I did meet a few children at church.

At that time my family was attending a little Baptist Church in Windom. There were two little girls there named Jo and Irene. I didn't get to spend a lot of time with them, but at home, I conjured up two imaginary friends named Jo and Irene. I had a lot of fun with them. I would show them the pictures I had drawn and tell them stories. We played dolls together and wherever I went, they went. It took me years to realize where I came up with those names.

I enjoyed going to church, and I especially

liked Sunday School. The teacher would give me a card each week that had a picture on the front and a Bible story on the back. One week it would be David and Goliath, another week, Daniel in the lion's den, and another week it might be Jonah and the whale. I always saved the cards, and when a little girl moved in nearby, she and I would get together and look through the cards and retell the stories. We had so much fun doing that, and it really stamped those stories into my memory.

One thing that emerged from the Great Depression was President Franklin D. Roosevelt's New Deal and programs like The Works Progress Administration (WPA). The WPA was a low paying, work-relief program that provided work to men and women in need and offered a way for people to live with dignity by earning the relief they received from the government. WPA employees built bridges, roads, public buildings, public parks, and airports. My dad went to work for them, and it was back breaking work. He had to take a heavy maul, which looks a lot like a sledgehammer, but with a wedge on one side (also known as a block buster) and beat rocks with it. They would put him to work on great big rocks, and he would have to beat them with the maul until they were small enough to use as gravel on the road. It was grueling work, but, as my dad always said, "It was a job."

To this day I don't know how he did it, but he would milk cows in the morning for a local farmer, then work all day breaking up rocks until late, and come back to milk the cows again in the evening. He would arrive home exhausted, and my mother was tired too, as she would work in the fields when she wasn't caring for the neighbor's baby or nursing a sick acquaintance. She would hoe the fields and pick cotton, or whatever was needed. Then she would come home, wash the clothes by hand in a washtub, and prepare a meal for my dad and me. I never saw anyone work any harder than those two, and somehow, we always had enough.

Some of my earliest and best memories are of Mamma Cason coming to visit. She would come for a month to three months at a time, and would bring her big trunk, a chair, and a bed. She had to bring her own bed because we didn't have an extra one, but we did have an extra room. When Mamma Cason came, I got to sleep in the bed with her, and I loved snuggling up next to her. She would tell me stories and sing songs to me, and we would whisper in the dark until I fell asleep.

In Mamma Cason's trunk were all sorts of wonderful treasures. I always enjoyed hovering nearby to see what items she would bring out next. Sometimes she would bring out her sewing items and make me a rag doll. Other times she would bring out papers that had stories for children and pictures to color. On very special occasions, she would pull out a box of candy, and she would give me a piece. She seemed to always know just what a little girl would want. And she told the best stories; I could sit and listen to her for hours.

Mamma Cason was crippled, and she walked with a cane, but she did not let that stop her. She helped my mother cook, took care of me, and she made quilts. She made a quilt for Mama and Daddy, one for Uncle John, and one for Aunt Sallie. I loved to sit and watch her sew, and sometimes she would let me practice on a little scrap of fabric. Mamma Cason would also help by sweeping the yard. People back then would often sweep their yards down to the dirt near the house, to create a safe place for children to play and make it easier to spot snakes.

Looking back, I suppose the main purpose of Mamma's Cason's visit was to allow my mother to go work into the fields with my dad and help pick cotton. It took everyone working to make ends meet. My dad, Charlie, only went to school through fifth grade; then he had to quit and help his family earn a living. He was smart, though, and had a lot of common sense. He picked up a lot of knowledge by listening to people talk and by going to movies. If he ever had a dime to spare, his favorite thing to do was go to town and see a movie, and especially movies about the West. His favorite actor was John Wayne. Some of the westerns of that era were *Sagebrush Trail, The Lucky Texan, Wagon Wheels, West of the Divide*, and *Moonlight on the Prairie*. When my dad came home from the movies, he would tell me all about the characters and the plot. He could make it seem so real!

Although he had a limited education, my dad made sure that I had a good start. He used building blocks to teach me letters, and he told me quite a few stories. My mother was a good storyteller too. She went to school through seventh grade in Windom and she would often read to me. Even though my parents worked hard, I remember them spending time with me. And although they had very little, they were willing to give what they could to help others.

We didn't go to see doctors very often because it was too expensive, but also my parents did not have a lot of trust in doctors. One time when my mother (Ruth) was about nineteen, she was having a great deal of pain in her mouth and decided to visit a local dentist to have the tooth removed. The man was apparently a quack and failed to properly numb the area. My mom was in agony while he pulled the tooth, and she vowed that she would never go to the dentist again. It scared her to even talk about it. She kept that vow for many years. Her teeth become abscessed, painful, and filled with cavities, but she refused to see a dentist. Sometimes she was in so much pain that she would walk the floors at night moaning and praying. Many of her teeth were so rotten that they broke off even with the gums, and she was self-conscious about her breath because of the infection. But the memory of that one experience with the dentist was so powerful that she would not go back.

Finally one day, when my mother was about thirty years old, a friend named Nell Edwards came over and began telling Mama about a new dentist in Wolf City named Dr. McDonald. She said that he was very gentle and that people were coming from miles around to see him. She urged my mother to go see him and have her teeth pulled. My mother's nephew, Don Whirley, heard about this discussion and said if she would go, he would take her there and pay for it. She finally consented to see Dr. McDonald just to make everyone happy and find out if he could help her. Dr. McDonald only pulled three of her teeth on that first visit, but Mama came home smiling and happy and said she "didn't feel a thing." It took about four trips to Dr. McDonald's office to extract all of her teeth, because he would only pull three or four at a time. I have never seen a happier person in my life, than my mom was the day her last tooth was pulled. Some of the teeth must have surely been very difficult to remove, as there was nothing left above the surface. Even though my mother was still a young woman, she was content to go through life without any teeth rather than continue to suffer the way she had. She never got false teeth, and over time her gums became very tough, so that she could eat whatever she wanted.

I think that must have made a deep impression on me, because I have tried to take good care of my teeth, and I always notice when people have a nice smile, and white, straight teeth. Even now, at eighty-eight years old, I still have most of my teeth, and I have never had a bridge or worn false teeth of any kind.

[1] Pigott, Kelly. Texas State Historical Association. Fannin County.
https://tshaonline.org/handbook/online/articles/hcf02

Eliza Deborah (Mamma Cason)

Me with my Buster
Brown haircut

John, Sallie, and Charlie Abner Cason (my dad)

SARAH LOUISE

When I was three years old, Mama and Daddy had another baby and named her Sarah Louise, but most of the time we called her Louise. She was born on May 21, 1934. I know my dad was really hoping for a son to help out in the fields, but they were just thankful Louise was alive. When she was born, they said she was "blue." Doctors know now that this condition is likely caused by a reduced amount of hemoglobin in the blood that carries oxygen throughout the body. When the baby is not getting enough oxygen, the skin turns blue. It gave my parents a scare, but as Louise grew, she seemed healthy and full of energy to me, but, of course, I was a child.

My family was living on Mr. Chaney's

place at the time, and my dad was the only person working the land. Mr. Chaney was unhappy about that, because he wanted a tenant with a large family, so there would be more people to work the land. He basically kicked us out, because he wanted a "larger work force," as he called it. So my parents moved us to the Johnson Place way down by Allen's Chapel. My dad didn't want us to live there, because it was pretty isolated, but it was all he could find. The windows on the house were very close to the ground, and there were often cows grazing nearby. The cows would come right up to the windows and look in. It was very unsettling to look up and see cows staring at you, and it scared my mother.

By the time I was four years old, I thought I was big, and I loved having a little sister. It was so nice to finally have a playmate. I had fun telling Louise stories and keeping her entertained, while my mother worked around the house, cooking and cleaning. One thing I noticed was that Sarah Louise seemed to have an unusual amount of accidents. She would fall a lot and hit her head on things around the house. One day when Mamma Cason was visiting, she took a bath and left the tub full of water. Somehow, Louise managed to fall into it.

Mamma Cason pulled her out, and Louise seemed to be okay. Once she fell and hit her head on a chair that left a cut on her forehead. Another time she fell against the stove. I noticed the falls, but I just thought that was what little kids did.

As Louise grew, she and I played all sorts of games together. We would run and play until I was completely worn out, but Louise would want to keep playing. When Louise finally got tired, she would sit in her little rocking chair and sing,"da-da, da-da" as she rocked to the tune of *There's an Old Spinning Wheel in the Parlor.* One year for Christmas, Louise got a little red wagon, and I got some blocks. She and I would load all the blocks into the wagon and haul them around the house or take them outside; then we would spend some time building dollhouses or whatever came to mind. Besides building blocks, we played chase, dressed our dolls, and played barbershop, where we pretended to cut each other's hair. Louise was very sweet and good-natured. One time when everyone was seated at the table, ready to eat, Louise came around and kissed each one of us. No one put her up to it; that was just her personality.

Occasionally, a peddler would come by

selling his wares. He had a wide variety of merchandise that he hauled around in an old pick-up truck. Louise and I loved to run out to the truck and look at all the pots and pans, toys, tools, and home remedies. Our mother would come out, too, and if she had any money at all, she would buy Louise and me a red sucker. We were so happy to get that treat, and we would make it last as long as we possibly could.

One time when Mamma Cason came to visit, she brought Louise and me each a new dress that she had made for us. My dress was light blue and covered in little flowers. Louise's dress was white with red circles all over it about the size of a dime. I remember that I really liked Louise's dress better, and I wanted mine to look like hers so bad, but I didn't say anything about it. I knew Mamma Cason had put a lot of work into those dresses, and I didn't want to appear ungrateful.

While we were living at Allen's Chapel, Louise became ill. She starting having chills and going into convulsions. She was probably having seizures, but no one knew what to do for her. My dad took her to see Dr. Leeman, who said she had congestion. He gave her Groves Chill Tonic (for chills) and a cold remedy called Three Sixes for general purposes. The Three Sixes was very bitter, and who in their right mind would give a medication the name 666? One night Louise was shaking so badly that my mom and dad kept her in the bed with them all night. The next day my mother got a ride from a neighbor and took Louise to a "rubbing doctor" named O'Neal. He said her "bowels were locked," and he performed some chiropractic adjustments. Sarah Louise died in his office. My mother held Louise's body in her lap all the way home. When Mama came inside the house, she laid Louise's little body out on a board between two chairs.

I was only five years old, and I couldn't understand what had happened to my little sister and playmate. People came over to the house and talked quietly to my parents and looked at Louise's body, so still and quiet on the board. They looked at me sadly and patted me on the head, and some would just shake their heads. Then my parents told me I could kiss Louise on the head and say goodbye. I did, but I still didn't understand. No one talked to me about my little sister; no one explained to me that she had died, or why; I was so confused.

There was a road that ran between Windom and Honey Grove and about halfway between the two communities, there was another road that ran north to Allen's Chapel. At the end of the road was a little cemetery, and that's where they buried Sarah Louise. It was such a sad day for all of us. After that, my mother could not stand the thought of staying at Allen's Chapel, so we moved back to Chaney's Place. Every time we had to pass by Allen's Chapel, my mother would get tears in her eyes; she missed her baby so much. We all missed her.

I'm surprised that Mr. Chaney allowed us to move back into his place, but I think his conscience must have been bothering him. Or maybe he thought my mother would be able to help in the fields, since she no longer had a baby. Whatever the case, that's what she did. She would go into the fields and hoe, pick cotton, or whatever was needed. My dad needed the extra hands, but I'm sure my mother was grateful for something to keep her mind off her loss, temporarily. Maybe the hard work helped her process what had happened to her baby girl.

Now I was an only child, again. I went back to playing with imaginary friends, storytelling, and drawing. Meanwhile, my Aunt Sallie started attending East Texas State Teachers College (currently called Texas A&M - Commerce) to become an educator, and my Uncle John met a young woman named Earlene and married her. He and Aunt Earlene had a little girl named Deborah. As if by divine appointment, Uncle John and Aunt Earlene moved in just a little way up the road from my family. Deborah was only three years younger than me, and we became good playmates. Sometimes when she came to visit, I would hide my doll from her, because I was afraid she would break it, but in many ways, my cousin, Deborah, helped fill the void created in my life after the death of little Sarah Louise.

Sarah Louise Cason

PICKING COTTON

My mother's side of the family, the Whirleys, were not as involved in our lives as the Casons. My Mamma Whirley died when I was only three, but I do remember her. In addition to my mother, Ruth Lavandie, she and Pappa Whirley had a daughter named Icie Faye, who suffered from mental illness and lived at home with them. Icie Faye had a son named Donald (Don), and he lived with them as well. They also had a son named Joe, who was very nice. He and his wife, Verdie, ran a restaurant, and they didn't have any children. When Verdie died, Uncle Joe married a woman named Vera.

Unfortunately, not all the relatives on that side were as kind as Joe. Icie Faye's son, Don, was cruel to me. He was abusive, and his behavior left its mark on my tender emotions. He must have suffered from some sort of mental illness like his mother. He would do horrible things to me. I was afraid to tell anyone for fear of what he would do the next time he saw me. It was my first introduction to how unfair life can be. Until that time, I had thought that if I treated people kindly, they would be nice to me. It was really hard to live with those painful experiences and not be able to talk to anyone about it.

About that time, one of my cousins gave me a schoolbook, and I loved to pretend I was reading it. When I "read" aloud to the family, my dad, Pappa Whirley, and everyone in the room would laugh and clap their hands for me. I felt like they were making fun of me, so I got to where I didn't like people to clap for me. People didn't always believe me, but I really didn't want them to clap. One time I was asked to recite a speech at church for Mother's Day, and I became very worried that there would be applause. I went up to the lady in charge and said, "I'll say my speech, but please, don't let them clap for me." The woman was very kind, and she agreed that she wouldn't let the audience clap. So, I recited the speech. When I was finished, some teenage boys starting clapping. I looked at them and said angrily, "I told you not to clap!" I sat down and got as close to my mother as I could. I was so mad at them for not respecting my wishes.

Growing up with a mentally ill sister, had an impact on my mother. She spent most of her life caring for people, and she seemed to have a gift for it. She often took care of sick people who lived nearby. One time she sat with a woman who was having a baby and helped with the delivery, and naturally, she took care of her own children when they were sick. Another time, Pappa Whirley was sick with pneumonia, and Mama was there for him. Later in life, he had a stroke. Through all of that she cared for him.

There was also a young woman who lived near our family, who had a baby. This girl was not prepared to take care of a child, and, besides, she wanted to hold a job. The baby was basically neglected when the mother was at home. The girl would put her in a room and leave her alone except for necessities. My mother saw what was happening, and she began caring for that baby. She would babysit her while the mother went to work, and she went out of her way to help the young woman and her child in any way she could. Whenever Mama heard of anyone who was sick, she wanted to find a way to help them. She never expected anything in return. I really think she should have been a nurse. If anybody ever had a natural talent for nursing, she did. It seemed like she was happier doing that than anything, even when she needed treatment herself.

When I was seven years old, Mamma Cason, Eliza Deborah Hickey Cason died of a cerebral hemorrhage; that was on November 29,1938. Her passing was a great loss to me. She had been a strong, positive presence in my life. After that, my parents put me to work in the fields picking cotton. I suppose part of it was practicality, since they no longer had anyone to take care of me, and because I was getting old enough to be useful.

When my dad first took me out into the field, he gave me a long sack to drag around with me that could hold 100 pounds of cotton. That first day, he showed me how to grab the cotton ball at the base and twist it out of the boll, being careful not to prick my fingers. Not all of the cotton was ready, so I also had to look for the bolls that were cracked open, exposing the white, fluffy cotton inside and leave the ones that weren't quite ready. Since the plants mature at different rates, the same field had be picked three or four times each season.[1] The quality of the cotton would diminish very quickly if it was left in the bolls too long, so we had to have a sharp eye, do a thorough job, and pick all the cotton that was ready. After allowing me a couple of days to get the hang of it, my daddy told me that I had to pick at least fifty pounds of cotton each day. It was the middle of July and boiling hot outside. I guess I wasn't meeting my quota, because my dad had to have a serious talk with me. He told me that if I did not pick fifty pounds of cotton the next day, he would give me a spanking.

The next morning, we got started early, and I worked all day in the hot sun. The work was hard on my back, and the burrs would prick my fingers, but I kept going. At the end of the day, we had to weigh our cotton, and my hands were scratched and bleeding from the sharp spikes on the cotton plants. When it was my turn to weigh in, I held my breathe. My bag was so full I couldn't even lift it. They put it on the scale and told me I had picked 49 pounds of cotton. It's hard to believe, now, that a little seven-year-old girl could do that, but I did! Unfortunately, I was a bit short of the mark. My father spanked me, but only a little. I know he hated to do it, but he didn't want to go back on his word. I think he was really proud of me.

From then on, anytime they needed me, I worked in the fields with my parents, unless school was in session. To this day, I get skin cancer (basal cell carcinoma) on my face and arms from all that time spent out in the hot sun. I also have emphysema and chronic bronchitis, and I read that respiratory problems can be one of the side effects of working out in the fields and breathing in all the dust and residue from the cotton. (Long-term exposure to cotton dust may result in excessive chronic annual loss in forced expiratory volume.[2])

I was very fortunate that I did not have to pick cotton when school was in session, because many of the neighboring children did. I was the only remaining child in my family, and my parents were determined that I would have a good education. One of my best friends was Virginia Crossland. Virginia would have to keep picking cotton with her family for about six weeks after school started, and then she would start to school late. I did my best to help her get caught up. We spent the night at each other's house quite a bit, and we get could get tickled so easily at the least little thing. Sometimes we would just look at each other and burst into peals of laughter. Everyone needs to have a friend like that.

Occasionally, on a Sunday afternoon, my family would pack a lunch and go for a picnic.

When this occurred, my aunts, uncles, cousins, and whoever could would join us. We often went to the local park, but one time we went to the Paris State Park for our picnic. As I looked around at all the people at the different tables, I thought everyone was together, one big, happy family. Now, I dearly loved deviled eggs, and we didn't seem to have any in our basket that day to go with the fried chicken, potato salad, and slices of watermelon. I was so hungry for deviled eggs, that I decided to look around and see if anyone else had any at their table. I wandered up to a nearby family, and there was a nice woman there. I sweetly asked her if she had any deviled eggs. The woman said, "Why yes, honey, we sure do!" and she gave me some. I was so happy to have them, and I took them back to our table. Aunt Sallie figured out what had happened, and she scolded me. I think she was a little embarrassed by it. But no one got too upset with me. Those outings were a real treat and a welcome break from the long, hot days in the cotton fields.

[1] Cotton dust exposure: Analysis of pulmonary function and respiratory symptoms. Lung India. 2017 Mar-Apr; 34(2): 144–149.
[2] Ganzel, Bill. Wessels Living Historic Farming: Cotton Harvesting. (2007). https://livinghistoryfarm.org

Uncle Joe Whirley and his wife, Verdie

That's me in the middle at a family picnic when I was about seven. Ruth Lavandie (Mama) is on the left, and my dad, Charlie, is on the right. He was very tall and lanky. Aunt Earline (Deborah Rebecca's mother) is holding a tea glass in the air, and Aunt Sallie is to her right. This photo was taken at the park in Honey Grove.

ADOLESCENCE

I was just eight years old when World War II broke out. At that time, my dad worked at Lamar Creamery in Paris, TX. His given name was Charlie, but there was some mix-up on the business forms, so his work papers said, *Charles*. Besides Lamar Creamery, he also worked at a plant in Greenville, TX and he continued farming. He would work for various farmers, plowing the fields and bringing in the crops by day, and milk their cows in the morning and evening. Once or twice he made a crop on the halves (sharecropping). The landowner would allow us to farm the land, and in return, we would give him a share of the crop. Most of the time, though, my dad was just working by the day. Looking back, it seems that he was basically a migrant farmer who followed the crops and went where the jobs were. Our family lived in Windom; then moved to Lone

Elm, then Spring Hill, back to Windom, on to
Pattonville, and back to Windom again. Some
of the farmers my dad worked for were Marvin
Luttrell, Mr. Self, Mr. Wheeler, and Mr. Smith.
Daddy was one of the hardest working men I
know.

When I was nine years old, I almost
drowned, and to this day, one of my greatest
fears is of water. I was visiting a girl named
Louise Solomon who was twelve years old, and
her family had a pond behind their house.
Louise had a little brother who was only six,
and we all decided it would be fun to use a
washtub as a boat and float out on the water.
Somehow, it was decided that I would go first.
Why I went along with this scheme I do not
know; I guess I trusted Louise since she was
older than me. I also do not know where the
adults were at the time.

Louise and her little brother held the
washtub while I climbed inside. They gave it a
firm push, and the tub began to float away from
the bank. I was still trying to get settled and
figure out where to put my feet and legs, when
the tub flipped over, and I fell into the murky
water and began thrashing around. I did not
know how to swim, and I quickly began to sink.
Louise and her brother had no idea what to do.

While I was fighting for my life, a thirteen-year-old boy came walking by and saw the problem. He rushed into the water, took me by the hand, and pulled me out. I was terrified, and I don't even know if I thanked the boy properly. I never saw him again, and I don't even know his name. He was my guardian angel. After that, I would never again go near a body of water.

At that time we lived at Lone Elm, where I was able to attend school with my cousin, Evelyn Whirley Anderson, and we became good friends. We would play together at recess, trade items in our lunches with each other, and sleep over at each other's house. Evelyn was eleven and I was nine. When the family moved to Pattonville for a year, we still wrote letters to each other. She was a nice person and a good friend, and as of February 6, 2015, she still lived in Bonham, Texas. Evelyn went on to marry Doyle Burtram, who passed away January 6, 2015.

I was eleven years old, almost twelve, before my mother and father had any more children. Finally, in the midst of World War II and the Holocaust, in 1942, they had twins, Lena May and Dorothy Faye. We were living in the country outside of Pattonville, and Dr. Robinson came to our house from Paris to deliver the babies. I was at my friend Maude Dee's house during the delivery, but once the twins arrived, I came back home and washed the sheets off of Mama's bed in a big tub on the porch. There was so much blood.

Lena May needed an incubator. She was fragile, and the doctor didn't expect her to live long. It is awful what they did, but they regulated our old iron cookstove, and put Lena May in it like an incubator. After a few days, Lena May started doing better, and Auntie came over with a bunch of her friends. They brought clothes and diapers for the babies. Two grocery stores went together and donated us a lot of food and milk. My dad got a job milking cows about a mile away, and the farmer would let him take some milk home. Everyone pulled together and helped each other.

My mother breastfed the babies as long as she could, but she didn't have enough milk for them both. Pretty soon they were taking bottles, and it was my job to help. We moved down to a place called The Hollow, and I went to school during the day, so Mama managed the babies by herself. I don't know how she did it. Dorothy Faye was much stronger than Lena May and could hold her head up and sit up straight at an early age, whereas Lena May could not. My parents began to wonder if Lena May was developmentally delayed. As the twins grew a little older, it became clear that Lena May was not thriving the way Dorothy Faye was. There was some concern as to whether my mother had received enough nourishment during pregnancy to meet the needs of two babies, especially given the fact that she had had prior issues with malnutrition. She was such a hard worker, and she always placed the needs of others ahead of her own. One thing is for sure, pregnancy took its toll on her, and deprived her own body of valuable nutrients. She developed severe osteoporosis and later in life became very stooped over from the waist. She never let that slow her down, though. She continued waiting on everyone and caring for all those around her throughout her entire life.

Having sisters changed everything for me. I was old enough to help out, and I took on a lot of responsibility for caring for them. When I came home from school each day, I knew that I was either going to be babysitting, washing dishes, helping to cook supper, washing clothes, or all of the above. When I would get close to the house, there was a pretty tree I liked to climb up into and just sit for a little while. I just wanted a little quiet time to myself before I had to start working, but pretty soon, Mama would stick her head out the door and call for me to come help. One time Auntie came to stay with us for a week, and I thought for sure that I would get to sleep late, but no such luck. My dad had to get up at 2:00am, so Auntie would get up and fix him breakfast, and she would wake me up too. There was always something to do, because just about the time you got one baby to sleep, the other one would wake up.

I learned how to change diapers and feed Dorothy Faye and Lena May. It was fun to have children in the house again, and it was no doubt good training for me. I had a little friend, Barbara Anne McDarrow, who lived nearby, and she would come over and bring her dolls. We had a lot of fun playing house with our dolls. Barbara Anne's family had a wagon, and if I was ready in time, I could catch the wagon and ride to school with them. They would stop and pick up several kids nearby, but if I missed the wagon, I had to walk about a mile to school. The teacher really liked me and was very nice to me. She liked it when I could come to school.

As the twins grew older, we played together and even though I was eleven years older than them, we were all very close. Lena May seemed a little shy around people, but otherwise, they seemed like any other set of twins.

Once my sisters started to school, it became more obvious that Lena May wasn't picking up on things as easily as the other kids. Still, no one really thought anything was wrong, and Lena May's teacher really liked her and spent a lot of time with her. Lena May loved her. We started to notice that Lena May didn't have very good social skills. She would get offended easily and didn't communicate well with others. She also had difficulty learning to read, but she could write her name. Still she didn't seem that much different until she got a little older. She developed this thing about photographs. She thought that all pictures should have eyebrows drawn on them. If she found a photograph, she would draw on eyebrows with a pen, even other people's photographs, if she could get her hands on them. And she loved the color red. She wanted everything to be red: her shoes, her dress, her fingernails, her socks, you name it. As she entered young adulthood, it became clear that she would not be able to cope on her own. There was an event that occurred in her life that traumatized her, and she never seemed to recover to the point that she had been functioning at before. She spent her entire life living at home with our parents until they could no longer care for her, and then she entered a nursing home. Two things she loved to do were listen to preachers on the radio, especially Bob Wilson, and she loved to sing. Sometimes she would walk around the housing singing hymns; one of her favorites was "I'll Fly Away," and she always enjoyed hearing other people sing as well. Lena May passed away at a nursing home in Sulphur Springs on July 27, 2016.

Dorothy Faye, on the other hand, thrived and married a kind and honorable man, George Frank Connor, and together they had four beautiful children. Dorothy Faye and I have always had a good relationship, and she and Frank helped me a lot over the years. They were very giving and thoughtful of others. Frank passed away on February 27, 2017. Dorothy lives in Sherman with her son, Charles Ray, and his wife, Kathleen, in the house that she and Frank built, and she still calls often to check on me.

Lena May (left)
and Dorothy Faye

Ruth Lavandie, Charlie
Abner, Mary Ruth,
Dorothy Faye and Lena
May Cason

Frank and Dorothy
Connor

43

ROBERT THOMPSON AND CONRAD THE COBBLER

The most influential man in my life was Reverend Robert Thompson (also known as Brother Thompson). When I was a senior in high school at Windom, Texas, he was attending Austin College and serving as an intern and acting pastor for several small communities in Fannin County. In this capacity, he had a strong impact on my emotional and spiritual development. The first time I ever met Robert, I was seventeen years old, and my family was living in a rent house. Robert was going around, introducing himself to people and had made an acquaintance with our landlord. They came walking down to the house together, and I noticed that Robert was quite young, probably in his early twenties, and very handsome. The landlord introduced him to my family and told us that Robert was going to be the local preacher for two weeks each month.

Now I had been raised a Baptist, but Brother Thompson was preaching at the Presbyterian Church. This created a bit of a dilemma for me, but I thought it over and decided to go with the landlord's family so I could hear Robert preach. Sunday rolled around and I found myself nervous and jittery inside. We arrived at church and I listened intently to everything he said. I liked him quite a bit, and I decided to keep going as often as I could. He had a way of relating the scriptures to our daily lives that made everything so real. I especially remember a story he told from the pulpit about *Conrad the Cobbler*. It was very touching, and I had tears rolling down my cheeks.

The story was about a man named Conrad who made shoes for a living. He was a very humble man and led a quiet life. One night the Lord appeared to him in a dream and said, "Conrad, I'm coming to your house today." The next morning Conrad jumped out of bed and started cleaning his house and preparing for the Lord's visit. He made a special pair of shoes to give to Jesus - the nicest he had ever made. He put milk, honey, and bread on the table, and when everything was ready, he sat down and waited for the Lord to come. As Conrad was waiting, he heard a knock at the door. He was so excited and thought that it must be Jesus at the door. He rushed to open the door, but saw that it was an old man with bleeding feet. When Conrad saw the man's feet, he knew that he had to help him. He said, "Lord forgive me, but I'm going to give him the shoes I made for you." And that's what he did. The man was so happy and grateful to get the shoes. Conrad sent him on his way and sat back down to wait for Jesus. Time went by and a woman came to his door. She was carrying a load of sticks on her back. She was stooped over and seemed tired, cold, and hungry. Conrad felt compassion for her and invited her to come in and warm herself by the fire. He fed the woman the bread and honey he was saving for the Lord and gave her the milk to drink. When the woman was rested, she went on her way carrying her load of sticks. Conrad had just settled back into his chair again to wait for Jesus, when he heard a sound outside. He leapt from his seat and rushed to the door. He just knew that the Lord had finally come! But when he opened the door, he found a little boy who was crying. Conrad talked to the little boy and discovered that he was lost. Conrad hated to leave, but he helped the little boy find his mother, and then he went back home to wait for the Lord. Conrad noticed that the sun was about to set, and still the Lord had not come. He cried out and said, "Lord, the day is almost over, and you haven't come yet. You said you would be at my house today!" Then the Lord spoke to him and said, "Conrad, three times I was at your door. I was the man with the bleeding feet; I was the woman whom you gave bread to eat; I was the boy on the friendless street. When you showed mercy unto the least of these, you showed mercy unto me."

That story made a lasting impression on me, and my respect for Robert Thompson increased even more. I had never met anyone before who had such a way of making the scriptures relevant to our lives. I continued going to the Presbyterian Church with our landlord and his wife when I knew Robert would be preaching.

My birthday is in September, so I turned eighteen right after the school year started, and

I was elected class president. We were busy with so many athletic and social events that the year seemed to fly by. As high school graduation grew near, our class needed to choose someone to speak at our commencement. The superintendent of the school district acted on his own and invited a former superintendent, Brent Tartar, to give the baccalaureate sermon. Mr. Tartar was an older gentleman and was the manager over Durham Homes (in Commerce) where the family was to live, later on. At that time, however, he was working at a college. The students in my class were respectful of his position but not very excited about being excluded from the decision making process, and we didn't really have any personal connection to him.

One day, after church, I was visiting with Robert and we began discussing the upcoming graduation ceremony. He asked me who the speaker was going to be, and when I told him it was Mr. Tartar, he said, "Oh, he's an older gentleman. You need someone younger." Well, that got me to thinking, so I said, "How about you? Why don't you give the sermon?"

Robert didn't commit either way, but he pointed out that there might be a conflict, since someone else had already been scheduled.

Since I was the president of my graduating class, I thought that perhaps I could persuade my classmates to invite Robert Thompson to speak. I began to talk to everyone about my idea. I talked to the student council, met with teachers, and essentially led a movement to get the speaker changed. Another student, Dolly Spelts, who also went to Brother Thompson's church, backed me up and told everyone Robert was a good speaker. The campaign was successful and the administrators agreed to let Robert Thompson deliver the commencement address. When graduation day finally arrived, Robert spoke to us about our plans for the future, and gave us many points to consider. I realized that although there were many ways he had helped me, I had also helped him. Now he could say that he had delivered a baccalaureate sermon.

A few weeks later, it was announced that Brother Robert Thompson would be holding a revival. I really felt led to go, like I just *had* to go, but I didn't know how to go about it. I didn't want to break away from the Baptist church that I had been raised in, but the revival would be held every night. I guess I felt that I was being disloyal, but I felt compelled to attend, so I did. Although the church where he preached was Presbyterian, it was more like a community church. There were Pentecostal people there, Baptists, Methodists and Presbyterians. That made me feel better about my decision. He preached a very moving sermon that first night, and when he gave the invitation, the musicians played, *I Need Thee Every Hour.* I responded to the altar call and went up front. Brother Thompson asked me if there was anything he could pray about with me. I told him that I wanted to rededicate my life to the Lord, and then we prayed together. He prayed the sweetest prayer.

After that, I starting writing Brother Thompson letters, and I would ask him questions, usually about moral issues or things that had come up in my Bible reading. He always wrote me back and gave me good advice. I left the area for one year to attend Draughn's Business College in Dallas. Robert wrote to me while I was there and encouraged me to follow my dreams of becoming a writer or a teacher. When I came home on the weekends, he would often come by and pick me up for church. He would say, "If you and your grandfather will meet me over there by the road, I'll take you to church and take you home afterward." My parents were still going to the

Baptist church, but my Pappa Whirley liked to go the Presbyterian church with me.

On one of these occasions, a woman from church, Verna Brewer, invited Robert to lunch at her house. She was very sweet and insisted that Pappa and I join them. Pappa was agreeable, so we all had lunch and spent the afternoon together. When the time was getting close for the evening service, Robert invited me to ride to church with him, and the others came on later. After church, he took Pappa and me home, and he made my entire family feel very special.

There was another young woman in the church named Jeanine Suder, who had been a classmate of mine in high school. Sometimes Robert would ask her to play the piano when he preached. He usually brought a girl with him from Austin College to play the piano and sing, but when he didn't have anyone, he would ask Jeanine to play. I'm ashamed to admit that on those occasions, I felt jealous of Jeanine. I was very fond of Robert, and it was hard to see my classmate getting extra attention. My feelings for him had grown to the point that I felt I needed to address them. It took me a while to decide the best way, but, finally, I decided to write him a letter and tell him how I felt about him. I don't remember the exact words I used, but I let him know that I admired him, and that I liked him a lot. He quickly wrote me back and said that he loved me in the Lord, and he very tactfully let me know that he was engaged to a "wonderful girl." He said, "She doesn't play the piano or sing or anything, but I feel that she is the one for me." I tried to be happy for him, but I was disappointed to learn that he was taken.

As I thought more about it over the next few weeks, though, I realized that my crush on Robert was probably because he was someone I looked up to and respected, especially after I had such a good experience under his ministry, and he seemed to pay special attention to me. Looking back, I realize he probably made everyone feel that way. I was able to accept that he was in love with someone, and I continued to hold him in very high esteem, but I lost track of him over the years.

I recently learned that Robert wound up living in Sherman, for twenty-seven years. I would give anything if I had known that he was so close. My parents lived in Sherman for a while, and my sister, Dorothy, also lived there with her family. I could have gone to hear him preach, if I had realized it. Sometimes I would think of him and want to find out where he was, but I didn't know how to go about it. All down through the years I have remembered Robert Thompson and the encouragement he gave me. He was the kindest, most influential man in my life.*

Robert Thompson passed away in 2009 after a brief illness. He was married to his wife, Betty Jo, for 56 years, and they had four children. I was sorry to hear of his passing, but I learned that he had a collection of sermons entitled, *Clay Pots.* I ordered a copy and read them all. I was so happy to get them. I could hear his voice as I read, and it was like having a part of him with me.

My senior photo

*See the dedication of this book for a poem that I wrote to Robert Thompson when I was in high school.

LETTERS AND HEARTBREAK

When I reached my full height, I was five feet, five inches tall and had long chestnut colored hair. Sometimes I would treat my hair with lemon juice or vegetable dye to make it lighter. I had clear blue eyes and a wide smile. I was friendly to everyone and had many friends in school. My teachers told me I should become a writer, and students respected me for my abilities. One time I wrote a poem about one of my teachers and gave it to him. Later, I helped a friend write a paper for college, and the professor told him it should be published.

I was reserved and held conservative values, but I loved to laugh and listen to people tell funny stories. Sometimes I would get so tickled that my whole body would start shaking, and I couldn't stop. I still enjoy being around people who make me laugh. When I graduated from Windom High School in May of 1949, my sights were set on becoming a writer or a teacher. As with many women of my generation, however, I felt torn. While I did enjoy writing, I also wanted to get married and have children and a happy home.

As I mentioned previously, I attended Draughn's Dallas Business College for one semester. My family didn't have money to pay for college, but my dad had a friend named Opal Posey, who lent me $50 to pay my tuition, and he would send me $20 each month for my expenses. (Later on, when I got married, Mr. Posey told me to forget about the loan. He said I could keep the money as a wedding gift.)

At Draughan's I roomed with Clarabelle. We were called "school girls," and people in the community considered it a privilege to have a school girl in their home. We paid our own tuition, but they provided room and board, and we took care of their children and did light housekeeping, like drying dishes. I thought Clarabelle and I were better friends than we really were. The money Mr. Posey gave me wasn't much, but it was enough to cover whatever I needed throughout the month. I did without some things, so that I could save up and buy Clarabelle a Christmas present. I managed to save fifteen dollars of my allowance and bought Clarabelle an elegant, pink housecoat for Christmas. When I gave it to her, she acted like it was nothing and didn't give me anything. I was really hurt by that. Looking back, though, I realize I was actually mad at myself. No one asked me to give Clarabelle a gift; I was the one who did it. My parents didn't get anything for Christmas, and that money could have gone a long way toward helping them. I wish now I would have thought of them first.

There were five of us girls who ran in a group at Draughan's: Clarabelle, Dorothy (not my sister), two girls from India, Vini and Anika, and me. I really enjoyed talking to the girls from India. They had interesting stories to tell.

I was no angel while I was away at college. I had a problem with boys. As soon as I walked in the front door, a boy fell in love with me, and he wouldn't leave me alone. A lot of the boys liked me. I'm not saying I did anything bad, but Clarabelle said I was a flirt. I wasn't trying to flirt; I just smiled at them. Clarabelle's brother liked me. I told her one day, "Your brother is so cute! I want to write to him. Does he like for girls to write him?" She said he did, so we started corresponding. I went out with him for a while, but I guess I wasn't his type.

I lived in three different houses while I was there. The first house belonged to a wealthy Jewish family. They owned a big drugstore and lived in a nice house near Dallas Lake. They had a little baby that I took for walks after school. The second family was a white family that lived in Dallas and owned Lloyd's five and dime store. They had two little boys, Stevie and Joe. Stevie was in diapers, and one morning before he went off to preschool, he came to my door wearing a wet diaper and holding a bottle in his hand. He said, "Sah-wy, Ma-wy, sah-wy." I said, "That's okay, lets get you changed," He was chubby and cute and so sweet. The third family was another Jewish family. The wife wore a big, square diamond, and she didn't want me to eat at the table with the family. They had a little girl, and she and I got along so well as long as the mama wasn't there. If the mother was home, that little girl would act out. It was obvious that she wanted to be with her mother, but the mom liked to go play bridge with her friends, and I guess she didn't want to have a child with her. The little girl would throw a fit, but as soon as the mama left, everything was fine again.

While I was at Draughn's, I took typing, business English, shorthand, and other business courses. I could already type, but at Draughns, I improved my skills. I don't know how I ever got into that shorthand class, but it was very complicated. Dorothy took a different kind of shorthand that was simplified, and it was so easy, but I had to work very hard to learn the style that I was studying.

I lived in Dallas during the week, but on the weekends I would go home to spend time with my parents. My dad was working for a farmer by the day. When I came home on the weekends, I still went out into the fields and helped him work. Hoeing cotton was a good way to stay in shape and maintain your weight; I got down to 125 pounds.

During that time, my dad made a crop for Mr. Thurman Batey (on the halves) outside of Honey

Grove, and I helped him make that crop. We had a good deal going with Mr. Batey. He really took good care of us. Mr. Batey would come by every Wednesday night and take our family to church and take Mama and me to the Women's Missionary (WM) meetings with his wife. In addition, he would pick up our laundry on Saturday, take it to the laundry service, have the clothes cleaned, and bring them back. He also picked us up for church on Sunday mornings and Sunday nights. He was probably the best landlord my parents ever had. He was always doing nice things for us. One time he brought a big keg of ice water to the field where we were picking cotton. Sometimes he would bring cold Coca Colas. He liked Cokes himself, so he thought everybody else did. Boy, that was a treat!

Sometimes the farmers asked me to keep their books and make sure people weighed in their cotton crops correctly. I did that part time, and then I got a job for about a year working at American General Investment Corporation as an office worker. Young soldiers (G.I.s) would come there to get liens to purchase homes, so I had the opportunity to meet many new people, and I made friends with a young woman named Jean, who also worked in the office.

Around that time, I started going out with a man named Bob Tucker. He was very outgoing, and he had a gold tooth. I thought he was so handsome. I didn't have any experience with men, and I see now that I was very naive. I liked Bob quite a bit, but I could tell he was still in love with his first wife, Mildred. He had children with her, and when he would go to visit his kids, the ex-wife would flirt with him, asking him to zip up her dress and provocative things of that nature. She acted like she wanted him back, but she was already remarried. Meanwhile, Bob was talking to me about getting married. Church was an important part of my life, so I wanted anyone I dated to be a Christian. Bob liked gospel music, but I couldn't get him to go to church with me. Whenever I asked him to go, he would say, "I would have to cover up my face if I went in a church."

I decided that he wasn't really going to marry me, that he was just playing me. Even though I loved him, I wrote Bob a letter and broke up with him. I wrote, "I know that you don't really want to marry me. I hope you and your wife get back together, because I know you still love her." I gave him the letter, and that was that.

Well, the next thing I knew, my *friend*, Jean, came over to visit. She saw some pictures of Bob Tucker on the dresser and said, "You really loved him didn't you?" I said, "Yes." Then Jean told me that she and Bob were going to California to get married. I was stunned. Here I was trying to do the right thing and encouraging him to get back with his wife, and my friend had gone after him behind my back. I really felt betrayed.

While Jean and Bob were in California, I met a man named Charles Wesley (Pete) Holley. It was around 1950, and I was working at the mortgage company. My friend, Billie, and I were walking home from the drugstore one day, and this car pulled up beside us. Inside was Pete and his uncle, Leon; I had never seen them before. Pete introduced himself and started talking to me, and pretty soon he pulled out a ring from his pocket. He announced, "I said that whoever this ring fit, I was going to marry." He tried it on my hand, and it fit. Pete was tall and very good-looking and had dark hair. He looked like a young Elvis Presley.

I was still hurting from the break-up with Bob and his having married a woman that I thought was my friend. I was charmed by Pete's outgoing nature, so I started dating him, and Billie and Leon started dating. About a month or two later, Pete and I were married. Pete told me that he was unable to have any children, because he was sterile. I'm not sure how he knew that, but I didn't ask any questions. I wanted to have children some day, but we were already married. We rented a tiny space in a boarding house that had a small bedroom. It was only big enough for the bed and a chest-of-drawers. There was one tiny bathroom, and a combination kitchen and living room that just had a couch in it. My dad started working at Lone Star Gas Company to bring in some extra money, and he began staying with Pete and me throughout the week. So here we were, just getting started in a tiny little place, with my dad sleeping on the couch at night. It was not a very good set-up for young newlyweds, and Pete and I argued a lot. I even threatened to leave him within the first month.

While this was going on, Jean and I started writing letters to each other. One day there was a knock at the door, and to my surprise, there stood Jean and Bob Tucker at the door. It turns out they were looking for a room to rent, and they got one in the very same place where Pete and I were living. That just added insult to injury. By this time, Jean was pretty far along in a pregnancy, so I helped Bob move their furniture and other stuff upstairs. While we were alone in their apartment, Bob said to me, "You really surprised me, getting married." I said, "Well you surprised me too!" Later, he said to me, "I'm sorry you got such a bum deal." Apparently, that was his way of apologizing, but I thought to myself, "Who do you think you are?"

A few weeks went by, and Pete and I were still not getting along very well, and we had very little privacy. One day Pete said to me, "You didn't really mean it when you said you were going to leave me, did you?" Well, something else happened, I guess another argument, and that was it for me. I got my things together while it was still dark and left the house. I went to my cousin's house, and left a note for Pete. Of course, my dad was still there, sleeping on the couch, when I left.

Later my dad told me that Pete was sick when he realized I was gone. He was so weak he could hardly carry his suitcase. Then my dad set out to find me, so Bob Tucker took him all around in his car to look for me. Wasn't that crazy? The man I had fallen in love with was helping my dad look for me, so he could take me back to the man I had married. Everything was so messed up.

That night, Pete came back to the apartment to get the rest of his things. Meanwhile, my dad was planning to go home to Windom, and I wanted to go with him, so my cousin and his wife took me back to the apartment to gather my things. Pete's brother-in-law, Don Cason (no relation to my family) showed up, and Pete adopted a very cocky attitude in front of him. We really didn't have much to say to each other.

Pete and I were only married for about four months, but I heard from Pete's cousin and other people that he was having a difficult time getting over me. Pete's mother wrote to me and said, "I sure am sorry about you and Pete's trouble." When I look back on the situation, I know that, really and truly, I just didn't love Pete. Unfortunately, I married him on the rebound from Bob Tucker. Bob got married, so I wanted to get married too, and Pete came along at just the right time with that ring. I have always felt regret about the way it ended, though. I should have talked to Pete and told him how I was feeling, instead of writing him a note and leaving the way I did.

Pete Holley, also known as Pete C. Holley and C.W. Holley, is 83 years old and lives in Rosston, Texas with his wife Vera (as of February 2015). I contacted him recently, just to check on him and to apologize. I wrote him a letter to say that my leaving him was a "childish thing to do." I said that I shouldn't have done it, and that I was sorry that I did. I had been feeling that I just needed to tell him that. Well, Pete didn't seem to understand that I was trying to apologize. He was not interested in renewing any kind of friendship and seemed irritated by my contact. He wrote me back and told me that he was married. He said, "I don't want you meeting me somewhere, causing trouble," and he asked that I not try to contact him again. I was only reaching out in friendship and had no motive beyond that.

One good thing did come out of the letter, though. I had been worried that I had caused him a lot of heartbreak. When he wrote me back, telling me to leave him alone, I learned that he is happily married. That was a big relief to me - to know that he found someone to love, and that they had been together for fifty years! Pete said they were involved in church, and the church people really loved them. That also made me very happy.

This was taken when I was attending Draughn's Dallas Business College

This is me with my first husband, Charles Wesley (Pete) Holley.

I didn't tell my children about this marriage for a long time. I didn't want them to think less of me or to think that divorce was the answer.

MARRIAGE

Shortly after I divorced Pete, I started attending the Assembly of God Church in Honey Grove, Texas, and I worked at the local cotton mill, where I met a lot of new people, both men and women. I wasn't ready to date anyone, and I told everyone at church and at work that I would never marry again. The church frowned on divorce, and they frowned even more on remarriage. I really meant it when I said I was going to stay single.

There were two young men who worked at the cotton mill with me, and they both liked me. One was nicknamed Burrhead, and he and his friend would come around and talk to me daily. They knew I wasn't going to marry again, but they wanted to be friends. Burrhead would bring me a cold Dr. Pepper every day. He would just hand it to me, and if I was cutting thread off the quills, he would stop and help me. He was so nice. My bosses would help me too, sometimes. They would start talking to each other right beside my station, and pretty soon, without even seeming to realize what they were doing, they would reach into their pocket, pull out a pocketknife, and start cutting off the quills.

There were some good-looking boys there at the cotton mill. A very handsome young man named Joe Clayton started talking to me, and I could tell he liked me a lot. He had a broad forehead, and his hair was curly on top. He had a good build, and the cutest smile. I liked him quite a bit. He told a friend of mine that he wanted to go out with me, but he didn't know if I would say yes or not. Even though I had previously made up my mind about men, I became interested in him, and I wanted to go out with him. I just wasn't sure how he felt about me, and I was afraid to tell him how I felt. Maybe my troubles with Pete were a little too fresh on my mind.

Every morning when Joe came in to the mill, he would say to me, "Mary and that blonde hair." Between the lemon juice and vegetable dye and walking to work in the sun, my hair got pretty blonde in the summer time. And sometimes Joe would say, "I saw you crying in the chapel," which was a line from a song written by Artie Glenn and recorded by his son, Darrell Glenn (and later by Elvis). I don't know why he would always sing that song around me; maybe because he knew I was a Christian.

Whatever the case, one day I was sitting in a restaurant in Bonham with my friend Robbie, and I started telling her about Joe. I said to her, "Oh, you ought to see this boy at work. His name is Joe Clayton, and he wears this blue checked shirt and jeans, and he's built real good." Robbie looked up at me and said, "Is that him coming in the door?" I looked around and there he was, walking in the door. He came over and sat down by us and started talking. That made me feel so good, and I thought about him a lot. He was very good looking, and when he smiled, he was even better. To me, he was perfect! But I was kind of afraid to go out with him. I was worried about what his expectations might be, since I had been married before.

As I brought up Joe's name more around other people, I began to find out more about him. At one time he was going with a young girl named Linda Darling. I don't know if they were going steady or not, but he was also real good friends with a woman named Florence, who was at least 40 years old with grown children. I wasn't sure what kind of relationship he had with Florence, but I did become more cautious about what he might expect from me if we were to go out. There was also another woman who was twenty-seven and part American Indian, and he was good friends with her as well. I hope they just thought of him as a good friend or in Florence's case, a son. At any rate, he never did get up the nerve to ask me out. I think he knew I was too straight-laced for him, and I had serious reservations about him as well. He might have wanted a little more from me than I was prepared to deliver. But he sure was handsome; I believe he was what they call a ladies' man.

One night at church, sometime in 1953, I met a man named Dalton Philips. He was a World War II veteran, and he came up to me after an evening service and shook my hand. He was of average height and build and had dark red hair that was thinning, and he was quite a bit older than me. He kept coming to church, and pretty soon he asked if he could take me out. I wasn't really attracted to him, so

I turned him down. Besides, I still didn't plan to ever marry again, so I didn't see the point in dating. Dalton kept trying to persuade me to go have coffee with him and *just talk*, but I didn't want to. I found out that he had been married twice, and that did not improve my opinion of him. He drove a Nash car, and somehow he won my father over. My dad thought Dalton hung the moon. In fact, both of my parents encouraged me to get to know him. I guess my daddy was impressed with that new car. Maybe my parents thought he had a lot of money and would be a good provider. I don't really know why, but everyone was telling me that I should go out with him.

There were two girls in the church at Honey Grove at that time named Joanne and Jeanetta Cole who, like me, were in their early twenties. My friend, Robbie Boehler, and I used to go home with them nearly every Sunday after church, and we would have the best time together. Meanwhile, Dalton would go home after church with my mama and daddy, hoping to see me. Thanks to a little help from my friends, it just so happened that I was never home when he was there. The truth is, I didn't want to be there; I was afraid Dalton would ask me to go for a ride in his car or something like that, and I just didn't want to. He seemed like a nice enough man, but I didn't like him as a boyfriend, and I definitely did not want to go out with him. Mama and Daddy just kept telling me how great he was, and the pastor's wife thought he was "so great" too. They would all tell me that he and I would make such a good couple. Another woman in the church thought that too. Everyone kept putting pressure on me to give him a chance.

In spite of my attempts to avoid him, Dalton was very persistent and continued to chase me. Everywhere I would go, he would turn up, even in the store where I worked. He would come in like he was looking for something, but he was really there to see me. One day when I was walking to work, he came driving by. He stopped me and wanted me to go to Tommy Doyle's Restaurant in Honey Grove to eat a chicken fried steak. I tried to get out of it, but I hated to be rude, so finally, I accepted. Apparently, he took that as a sign that I was ready to date him. He kept coming around, so I told him we needed to have a talk.

We met in another restaurant the next day, and I told Dalton that I had been married and didn't want to get married again. I basically let him know that he should stop pursuing me.

He said that was okay, that we didn't have to get serious; he just wanted to go out. We continued seeing each other and would go out to eat or riding around. He started showing up at Mrs. Mitchell's house, where I lived with my friend Robbie, at 12:00 every day. I worked all night at the cotton mill, so I went in at 10:00 at night and got off work at 6:00 in the morning. When I was walking home, it was still dark. Sometimes Dalton would show up at work and drive me home. He said he was worried about me walking alone in the dark. Then he started showing up every day while Robbie and I were eating our lunch together. As soon as I was finished eating, he would always want to go somewhere. It seemed like I couldn't have any time alone or with my friends without him being there.

One time Dalton got mad at me, because I chose to help out a friend instead of going with him. I had told Jeanetta that anytime she wanted to look for a job to come get me, and I would go with her. Any time. A few days earlier, the heel had broken off of my shoe, and both of my shoes were covered with mud. Dalton took the shoes to have the heel replaced and had them cleaned for me. He made a date with me to bring the shoes back, and he planned to take me out to eat. Well, that's the day Jeanetta showed up and wanted to look for a job. I went with her, because I had given her my word, and she had come all the way from Honey Grove to Bonham. So when Dalton came, he was mad that I didn't go with him. Nevertheless, he brought my shoes back after that, all cleaned and repaired. He was still mad, but it didn't last long, and then he got in a good humor.

One night when he and I were out riding around, Dalton kept driving and driving and driving. I wondered where on earth we were going, and finally we ended up in Waxahachie, where he was living and going to school. That is when he asked me to marry him. I told him I didn't know if I should or not. I said I didn't know if I loved him that much or not. He said that I "would learn to love" him. I had been spending so much time with him, that getting married seemed like the natural next step; besides, all the other boys knew I was going out with him. I didn't know what to do. I thought to myself, "Lord, if I'm going to marry him, I need to love him more." I had some feelings for him by then, but it wasn't enough for marriage. Then the next weekend I was going home, and suddenly I realized that I was looking forward to seeing him. When I got home they told me that Brother Philips (as he was called by church members) was not there that weekend. He had gone to see his sister in Midland. I felt disappointed, and that is when I started to think that maybe I did love him, and pretty soon we were engaged.

When the young men at the cotton mill found out I was engaged, one of them said to me, "Mary Ruth, I thought you said you were never going to get married again." I said, "Well, I didn't intend to, but I changed my mind." He just looked at me and replied, "Well, that's your business," but I could tell that he was hurt. Just a day or two earlier, that same young man had given me a big box of candy. Also, Burrhead had given me a great big stuffed bear. They were clearly courting me, but they had respected my wishes and not tried to pressure me. They were really nice boys, and I could tell they were disappointed to learn that I was getting married.

On February 12, 1954, Dalton Dee Philips and I were married by Brother Simpson, pastor of the Methodist Church, at his home in Honey Grove. I was twenty-two and Dalton was thirty-five years old. We couldn't get married in our own church, because we had each been divorced, and our own pastor (Brother Hopkins at First Assembly of God) was unable to perform the ceremony for the same reason. After we were married, Dalton said to me, "I love you more than diamonds and rubies." He wasn't much of a reader, so I felt that what he said came from his heart, not from something he had read or heard someone else say. Another night he said to me, "I love you more than my own mother." From then on, I felt that I loved him, and I could never picture him being with anybody else.

Joe Clayton   Dalton Philips

Joanne and Jeanetta Cole

This is me after my
marriage to Pete

Dalton and me on our wedding day

MAMA

My mother was a beautiful woman with an olive complexion and fine, dark hair. She kept her hair very long and twisted it up into a bun most of the time. After she washed her hair, she would leave it down to let it dry. She and Daddy had a big fan in their house that didn't have a protective cover on the front. One day Mama got too close to the fan while her hair was down, and it got caught in the big, metal blades as they were spinning. Her hair started wrapping around the blades, pulling her head closer and closer to the motor. She was terrified. Mama cried out, "Jesus!" and suddenly, the motor quit spinning. Mama unrolled her hair easily and was not hurt. It was nothing short of a miracle.

When Dorothy Faye and Lena May were about fifteen years old, Mama became ill. She had been going to a doctor named Chancellor, who was pretty young and inexperienced. One day Mama passed out, and the pastor, Brother

Hopkins, carried her to the doctor's office. Dr. Chancellor examined her, asked her a few questions, gave her some medicine, and sent her home. Dalton and I were married, and he was still in school at Waxahachie Bible College, and we had our first child, Malinda Ruth. Shortly after Mama's fainting spell, our pastor's wife, Sister Hopkins, called and told us that Mama was ill and that we should come home as quickly as possible, so we loaded up and drove to Bonham.

When we reached the house, my mother could barely talk. Her face was yellow and very swollen. My father was sitting in the living room, and my Uncle Albert was there. My dad was afraid that if he called the ambulance, they wouldn't come. Dalton told him they would come and told him to go ahead and call the ambulance. While we waited, Mama would say, "Can't they hurry?" That's all she would say, and we could barely hear her. The ambulance arrived, but Mama was in very bad shape by then. When they wheeled her into the emergency room, the doctor on duty said, "What do they mean sending me a dead woman?" He was very plain-spoken and told us that he thought Mama had cancer of the liver. He said, "She needs seven pints of blood tonight."

The sister of a preacher friend offered to call the Army National Guard to try to get some help. Thankfully, the National Guard gave my mother the blood she needed. The doctor performed a transfusion, and it seemed for a while like she was doing better. Even though my Mother was gravely ill, Dalton wanted us to go back to my parents' house. Malinda was about six months old, and I was nursing her at the time; Dalton didn't like me nursing her at the hospital and insisted that I should be at home with her. I wanted to be close to Mama, but we drove back to my parents' house in Honey Grove.

While we were eating supper, the hospital called again, and said that my mother's body was rejecting the blood. We immediately drove back to the hospital. When we got there, many of the family were gathered around and most were very somber. Joe was there with his wife and his brother's wife. My cousin, Don, was there with his wife as well. Dorothy Faye and Lena May were kneeling down beside our dad, and everyone was gathered around Mama's bed, praying. Dalton and I joined them, and everyone prayed together quietly in their own way. While we were praying, my mother's condition began to improve, and the doctor determined that her body was starting to accept the blood. That was such a relief and a blessing. After she was no longer critical, the doctor diagnosed her as having malnutrition, and he sent her to Baylor Hospital.

I had a very good friend, Robbie Boehlor who lived near Bonham. When I first became friends with Robbie, I felt like God had a given me a new sister in place of Louise, a sort of honorary sister. Robbie and another friend drove me to Baylor to be with my mother. The doctors at Baylor said they found a tumor that they could not operate on. They did not do a biopsy, but they ran a scope down her throat and took pictures, and they took x-rays. They gave her a lot of vitamins and tried to build up her system. She recovered, but later on when she lived at Bonham, she had to go to the hospital again. She saw different doctors, and told them that the doctors had found an inoperable tumor. They doctors ran tests and x-rays and, again, said that she was malnourished. "But," they said, "we did not find a tumor. All we found was some scar tissue." The tumor was miraculously gone!

The doctors once again treated my mother for malnutrition by giving her vitamins and other supplements. They said she had Pellagra, one of the diseases seen in the prison camps during World War II. Pellagra is a serious digestive illness, usually related to a lack of niacin (vitamin B3).[1] One of the symptoms of Pellagra is dementia, which my mother did have later in life. I suppose it all goes back to when she was expecting the twins. My family was very poor, and my mother did not have proper food. Even though she was strong, carrying twins was hard on her and took a lot out of her body. Besides that, my mother sacrificed her own needs for everyone else. She would always wait on everyone at the table, and she would hardly ever sit down and eat anything for herself. By the time everyone was finished eating, there was hardly anything left. That is just the way she was. To compound the problem, she never got false teeth, so she couldn't chew food very well. In my opinion, all of this, coupled with not having good food available, probably led to the malnutrition.

In reality, my mother rarely got to enjoy the simple pleasures of life that many take for granted. One thing she really enjoyed was to get dressed up for church and have a pair of pumps to wear. She was an attractive woman and had a nice figure, but she wasn't vain. She just really liked pumps, and one time she was especially proud because she was able to get some pantyhose to go with her church outfit. She really felt dressed up then. There were many times my mother didn't get what she wanted, but she would take what she got and not complain. But she felt really dressed up in her pumps and pantyhose. I know my mother would have enjoyed having more nice things, as every woman does. But if you ever asked her what she wanted for Christmas or her birthday, she would say, "I don't know." We would usually end up getting her toiletries, a robe, a housecoat or something practical like that. My dad, Charlie, was not at all like her. He would just come right out and say what he wanted. One time, for instance, he told Dorothy Faye he wanted a watch for Christmas. Another time he said he wanted some boots, but Mama never would say. As I look back now, I would give anything if we had all gone in together and bought her a keyboard. She loved to play the piano, and that would have brought her so much joy. Even later, when she was in the nursing home, a keyboard could have offered her a creative outlet. That could have made a difference in her emotional well-being.

As it was, she was always giving of herself to others. She took care of my mentally challenged sister, Lena May throughout her life, until she and both my parents had to enter a nursing home.

As she began to age, my mother became very stooped over. (This was probably related to the malnutrition she suffered.) It started when the family lived in Bonham, but by the time they moved to Sherman, it was really bad. She was bent over from the waist and her shoulders were hunched over as well. Also, as she aged, her head leaned very far over to one side, and she could no longer hold it up straight. My dad, Charlie Abner Cason, died in a nursing home in Sulphur Springs, Texas at the age of eighty-one, on December 2, 1988. His funeral was held in Bonham and he was buried at Windom Cemetery. My mother, Ruth Lavandie Whirley Cason died on January 31, 1990 at the age of 83, also in Sulphur Springs. She was buried next to my dad at Windom Cemetery where they share a headstone.

---

[1] *Pellagra.* American Osteopathic College of Dermatology. https://www.aocd.org/page/Pellagra

P.O.W.

It's hard to imagine how my life would have been different if I had never met Dalton, if he had never pursued me, if people hadn't persuaded me to go out with him, if I had been more confident and expressed my desires more openly. In many ways, marrying him meant saying goodbye to my friends, my family, my church, my mentors, everything that I held dear. Although life with him was hard, I have seven beautiful children, and I am thankful for them all.

Dalton Dee Philips was born on February 13, 1919 in Stamford, Texas to Spencer Dee and Stella Malinda (Gee) Philips. Dalton had two sisters. The oldest was named Trentie Alice (known as Alice), and she marred Troy Avery (T.A.) McCarty, also known to the children as Uncle Mac. He was the CEO of Sharp Drilling Company. He and Alice were never able to have children, but they adopted a daughter, Stella Jerrice, who was born on

February 11, 1952, two days before Dalton's birthday and the same birthday as one of our children, Polly (in 1963). Alice and Mac had a housekeeper who did all the cooking and cleaning for them. The housekeeper became pregnant. (This was before Dalton and I were married.) I never knew who the father of the child was, but Alice and Mac adopted the baby and had the biological mom live in their home in the servant's quarters. Jerrice's mom continued to live with them and work for them as long as Alice and Mac were living, but the paternity of the child was never disclosed.

Dalton's other sister was named Dorothy Jo at birth, but she later changed her name to Jerrie and had a reputation for being very independent. Jerrie Philips made a significant contribution to the war effort and was mentioned in the Abilene Reporter-News on December 8, 1944. She graduated from WASP (Women Airforce Service Pilots) in Abilene, which trained women to be service pilots during WWII. General Arnold, the keynote speaker at the graduation, presented the graduating pilots with their wings and stated "the training of women as pilots is no experiment"[1] General Yount, another speaker at the event stated: "The training command not only was responsible for teaching the women pilots to fly military aircraft," he said, but also "utilized them throughout its nationwide network of flying and technical schools in more diversified assignments than any other command"' The paper also gives some personal information: "Miss Philips is the daughter of Mrs. Stella Edwards of Spade. She was graduated from Stamford high school and attended St. Mary's university at San Antonio. Prior to joining the WASPs, she worked in the advertising department of the San Antonio Express. A brother, Dalton D. Philips, member of the AAF, is a prisoner of war."

Jerrie Philips went on to marry Terry Badger, a pilot for the Marine Corps. Six years after the WASPS disbanded, Jerrie was sworn into the Air Force as a second lieutenant.[2] She was crushing barriers and stereotypes for women ahead of her time. Jerrie and Terry had five daughters: Kim, Jonie, Laurie, Holly, and Sharon Kay Badger. Little Sharon Kay died of leukemia, and in many ways, Jerrie was bitter for a while about losing her. She kept all of her clothes, and every year, on her birthday, she would have a party for her. Finally, Jerrie gave all of Sharon Kay's clothes to our children. At that time, Sarah was the right age and size to wear them. In 1977, members of WASP were granted military status, and in July 2009, President Obama awarded surviving WASP members the Congressional Gold Medal. Jerrie Badger traveled to Washington to accept her medal. [1]

When Dalton was very small, his parents, Stella and Spencer Dee, gave him a tricycle. He loved riding it so much, that his mother would think up excuses for him to use it. One day she sent him to the store on his tricycle to buy a package of wieners, so they could have hotdogs for lunch. When he got to the store, he forgot what he went for, and bought cheese instead. When he got home with the cheese, his mom said, "That's okay, we'll have macaroni and cheese!" Dalton and his little sister, Jerrie, each had a pet pig. They would run all around the yard chasing after those pigs.

Dalton could not see very well as he was growing up. He was nearsighted, and he had amblyopia (lazy eye) on one side. His dad didn't take his vision problem very seriously and said he would "outgrow it." Dalton worked hard and earned money, so he could buy glasses for himself.

In 1937, at the age of eighteen, Dalton

enlisted in the Army, Air Corps division, and served a four-year term. He was a Private First Class, and his serial number was 6278352.[3] His best friend in the Army was a fellow soldier named Roy Allen. They stayed friends all during their enlistment and after the war. Dalton met Roy's parents and he and Roy did everything together. They even made a pact to name their children after each other. When Roy had a son, true to his promise, he named him Dalton Earl. When Dalton had a son, he named him Allen Spencer, using Roy's last name instead of his first. Roy seemed a little disappointed by that, but he never said anything.

When Dalton's tour was over, he decided to reenlist. That was in 1941, before the United States entered the war. Dalton's unit, the 28th Bombardment Squadron, was sent to help defend the Philippine Islands as part of the Southwest Pacific Theatre. In September 1941, the 28th Bombardment Squadron became part of the 19th Bomb Group. On December 7, 1941 the Japanese attacked Pearl Harbor, and the next day, December 8th, they attacked Clark Field where Dalton's squadron was stationed in the Philippines "and practically destroyed the U.S. Army Air Corps' capability of conducting an offensive action against the enemy."[3] Because of this, they were a bombardment group in name only. All of their military maneuvers, such as they were, were conducted on the ground. (See the document *Military Leaders Who's Who* for a full account of everything that happened to the 28 Bombardment Squadron.)

On Christmas, 1941, they were ordered to go by train to Bataan. On December 29, they traveled to the port of Mariveles where they boarded a ship, the SS Maron, and headed for the Island of Mindoro. The Japanese spotted the ship and dropped six bombs on it without causing any serious damage. They continued their trip southward and the next day they learned that their sister ship, the SS Panay had been destroyed right where they were previously anchored. They sailed all night and arrived at the port of Bugo, Mindinao by morning. At Bugo the men of the 28th were issued "Enfield" rifles and taken by bus to Malaybaly. The next day they went by bus to the Carmen Ferry on the Pulangi River about 40 miles from the city of Davao where the Japanese forces were stationed. The men of the 28th Bombardment Squadron had orders to "guard the ferry and patrol the Pulangi River."[4]

On May 7, 1942 they were ordered to an area in Mindanao known as Alanib. At Alanib everyone had to turn in their rifles, and they were given shovels and food rations. Their orders were to dig trenches that would allow Filipino soldiers to guard a back trail used by the Japanese. When the men in the 28th were one kilometer from their destination, they were ambushed by a Japanese patrol. They had only shovels with which to defend themselves, and they lost a few men. They quickly backtracked to Alanib. When they arrived in Alanib, there were U.S. Army trucks waiting there. They thought help had arrived, but instead they learned that "all Armed Forces in the Philippine Islands had been ordered to surrender."[4] The trucks were actually there to take them to a prison camp at Malaybaly, Mindinao. Dalton D. Philips, Private First Class, is listed as one of the men who surrendered at Malaybaly. (Interestingly, many ranking officers were evacuated to Australia.) The conditions at Malaybaly, According to Dr. Jack Gordon's report, were better than many of the other camps. The men there were fed decently and had boots and clothes, but Dalton's squadron did not stay there long.

According to the Chikko Camp Report[5],

the Osaka Main Camp at Chikko opened on September 21, 1942. Dalton was taken there and is on the list of men who were held at that camp. Conditions at many of the camps were atrocious. Many of the men died in the prisoner of war (POW) camps from starvation, torture, sickness and disease and on the "Japanese hell ships" that took some prisoners to Japan. (See the Medical account by Jack Gordon, MD for a list and description of all the illnesses and conditions he treated among the POWs.)

When they first arrived at the POW camp, Dalton volunteered to be the cook for the prisoners, and the guards agreed to let him. All they had each day was a big pot of rice that had to serve all of them. If they happened to catch something, they would pitch it into the pot, anything that could be a source of protein. Dalton later told me that he lost a lot of weight while he was there, and that they nearly froze to death in the winter. At times his hands were so cracked from the cold that you could see the bone. The men each had one little thin blanket and had to huddle up together to try to get warm. Dalton said that many men were sick with pellagra, malaria, beri-beri, and other diseases.

The Chikko camp was made up of two one-story barracks that housed triple-decker bunks and measured 72' by 33', a two-story building, 72' by 30', (the bottom floor was a sick ward) and a fourth building that measured 64' by 30'. The buildings were made of wood and covered with stucco. There was a kitchen (30' by 30') that housed 8 brick ovens and a cement bath (10' by 10' that held 10 showers). According to the Chikko report, there was not enough space for the number of men held there. The Chikko Camp was bombed out on June 1, 1945, and on June 2 the prisoners were moved to the Tsumori Camp. This location was considered "unsafe," so on June 7, 1945, the prisoners were moved to Kita-Kukazaki. Chikko, Tsumori, and Kita-Kukazaki were all in the city of Osaka along the waterfront, which was a prime target for attacks. The purpose of placing the men here was "to provide workers for the docks."[5] They loaded and unloaded ships, worked in warehouses, loaded and unloaded railroad cars, and some of the men worked in clothing or food factories. Their workday was from 8:00a.m. to 4:00p.m. According to the Osaka report, during the three years the camp was open, the prisoners only received one-third of the supplies sent by the Red Cross. A typical breakfast was rice or soup, lunch was rice or bread with seaweed (which the workers carried with them to work), and dinner was rice and/or soup and once every 10 days they were given fish, according to a Japanese army doctor[5] however, Dalton said they had only rice to eat. Twenty-five men died at this camp from pneumonia, and/or beri-beri. The 28th Bombardment Squadron "distinguished itself during World War II, by being a part of the defense establishment in the Philippine Islands that disrupted the timetable of the Japanese Armed Forces in conquering Southeast Asia"[4].

After being liberated from the prison camp, Dalton returned to the United States. He and the other returning soldiers rode through town, and the people, especially women, were cheering for them and glad to have them home. Dalton reconnected with his best friend, Roy Allen, and one time they went to stay at a very nice hotel resort with another friend, Gene. Dalton caught a big fish and asked the chef at the hotel restaurant to cook it for him. He and his friends ate the fish, and then gave the restaurant what was left of it. When his second term was up, Dalton did not enlist in the Army again.

There was a woman he met while he was in the service. Her father was a pretty high-ranking military official. After his release they got married, but the marriage didn't last long. Later, he married another woman named Thelma, who already had two daughters. They did not have any children together and were soon divorced.

A short time later, Dalton began attending Southwestern Assemblies of God Bible College in Waxahachie. Meanwhile, I had started attending the Assembly of God church in Honey Grove. I caught his eye, and the rest, as they say, is history.

---

[1] Jerrie Philips, WASP graduate: Abilene Reporter-News, Abilene, Texas, December 8, 1941.

[2] Palmer, Audrie. *Love of flying drew Midlander...WASP.* Midland Reporter-Telegram: October 8, 2011.

[3] National Archives: Access to Archival Databases; https://aad.archives.gov

[4] Philippine Islands. U.S. Army Center of Military History. https://history.army.mil/brochures/pi/PI.htm (updated 3 October 2003).

[5] Osaka (Chikko) Camp Report: http://www.mansell.com/pow_resources/camplists/osaka/chikko/warcrimes_report.htm

Dalton with his mother, Stella Malinda

Dalton Dee Philips (after WWII)

Daughter of the Depression

Sharon Kay Badger

Jerrie Philips Badger

Dalton and me

MY CHILDREN

When Dalton and I were first married, we had a little purebred feist named Cricket. He was a small terrier, and we treated him just like a baby. When Dalton's mother, Stella, came to visit, she would bring gifts for Cricket. One time when Cricket was sick with something similar to pneumonia, Dalton and I laid hands on him and prayed for him. We rubbed Vicks Salve on his chest, wrapped him in a blanket, and nursed him back to health. He provided a lot of comfort during those first few months of marriage when everything in my life was changing.

After several months had passed, I began to think that I wasn't going to be able to have children. Finally, around the fifth month, I realized I was expecting a child. Unfortunately,

I had a miscarriage during the first trimester. That was in 1954. With my second pregnancy, I carried the baby to term, and on August 19, 1955, Malinda Ruth was born. She looked like a little doll. We dressed her up in the cutest clothes, and we both doted on her. Dalton had been reading a book by some psychologist about childrearing, and taking the author's advice, he decided that we should never tell Malinda *no* and indulge her every whim. Well, that didn't work out very well. She learned very quickly that she could always get her way, and her behavior became a problem. Then Dalton took the opposite approach and became very strict on her.

A little less than two years after Malinda's birth, on September 18, 1957, our son, Allen Spencer was born. I was so happy to have a boy. It seemed like everything was perfect, but there were signs of tension in our marriage. Just a few months later, I discovered that I was pregnant again, but my body wasn't ready to carry another baby. After all, I was still nursing Allen. I had another miscarriage during the first trimester. Both miscarriages occurred at home without treatment from a doctor, but I was able to verify that I had indeed been carrying a child.

By this time, our home life had become quite tense with Dalton being very strict on the kids, and I had found out some things about his past that were troubling. Some incidents had also occurred within my own family that made me realize he was not the person I thought he was. I threatened to leave him. I talked to my parents about it, but they said that we could not move in with them. They were still caring for my sister, Lena May, and they didn't have room for me and two small children. When I told Dalton I wanted out of the marriage, he showed me his true colors. He said that he would get his sister, Alice, to hire him a lawyer, and that I would never see my children again. I believed him, and I was terrified. Looking back, I don't know if Alice would have helped him or not, but at the time, he was very convincing. I knew that Alice's husband, Mac, was an important figure in the oil industry in West Texas, and they certainly had more money and resources than we did. Once I gave in and stayed, Dalton pretty much knew that he had complete control over me.

In 1959, I became pregnant for the fifth time and this time I carried the child to term. On October 22, 1959, Mary Deanna arrived. She was born with strabismus, and had to wear glasses at a very early age. She was so cute, barely old enough to sit up, and wearing her little glasses.

After that, Dalton and I had four more children: Rebecca Charlene, born October 9, 1961, Polly Ann, born February 11, 1964, Sarah Margaret, born May 4, 1965, and Dorothea Alicia, born December 16, 1967. I loved all of my children, and I wanted to be a good mother. My greatest desire for my children was for them to be successful and fulfill their dreams. Having lived through the Depression, I had an overriding fear of being without basic needs, yet I was satisfied, even when we had very little. I didn't have an income of my own or a budget to work with. Dalton was the only wage earner, and he paid the bills and bought the groceries. Even though things were tight, I found ways to economize. One thing I did was collect S&H Green Stamps from the grocery store. Every time we bought groceries, they would give us stamps that we could redeem for merchandise. When I saved up enough stamps, I was able to order little things I wanted for the house, usually cooking utensils, linens or kitchen gadgets. As long as I could feed my family, and they had clothes to wear, I was content.

We lived in Commerce, Texas until 1966 and attended First Assembly of God Church in

Commerce until 1972. Reverend Lee Alexander (1932-2000) and Mrs. Lavinia Hearington Alexander (1934-1990) were our pastors. They pastored in Commerce for thirty-two years. They were very kind to our family, and their sons Danny and David were good friends with Allen. The first day the Alexanders came to the church, Danny and David were wearing little bowties, and Allen, who was only five, said to them, "I like your bowties." They seemed to really enjoy that. Pretty soon, they felt like an extension of our family. When Brother Alexander went around visiting the sick or taking care of church business, he wore dress pants and a white, short-sleeved shirt. But on Sunday morning, or whenever he preached, he always wore a suit and tie. Things were more formal back then than they are now.

There was a man in our church that everyone called "Uncle Johnny," but his name was Johnny Radcliff. He always wore a white shirt and a pair of white overalls and wire-framed glasses. He lived alone and didn't have any family, but he was a tremendous blessing to the church. Every week he would mow the church lawn. You could always depend on him. Nowadays, people want to get paid for something like that, but Uncle Johnny did it out of love. He had a servant's heart. Dalton liked Uncle Johnny a lot and felt sympathetic to his situation. One day he invited Johnny to our house for lunch on his birthday. I cooked a good dinner for him and baked him a big chocolate cake. Uncle Johnny was so surprised and appreciative. He stayed at the house all day visiting with the family. Dalton really went out of his way to make Johnny feel like he had a family, and that meant a lot to Johnny. Uncle Johnny passed away before we left the Commerce church.

Our children all grew up going to church and Sunday School every Sunday. There was a framed picture in the church of Jesus carrying a little lamb. When Allen was just learning to talk, he used to point to that picture and say, "Look, it's Jesus and the 'abbit." I always thought that was so cute! And when Becky was just two years old, she would try to sing the hymns she learned in church. Instead of "I shall, I shall, I shall not be moved," her version came out, "Isha, Isha, Isha moo..." and she would clap her hands as she sang. That always got me tickled.

Back then there was a Baptist preacher in town, named Brother Gilmore, who had a radio broadcast. He would sometimes come by and pick up the older children and take them to the radio station with him and have them sing on the show. It was usually just Allen and Malinda, but one time Mary Deanna, Becky, and Polly got to go too. Sarah stayed at home with me, and we listened to the show on the radio and got to hear Malinda and Allen sing a special. People in the studio audience had to be very quiet. Polly was only three years old, but she sat there as quiet as could be. She was a good example of how disciplined the children were. Later Brother Gilmore commented to me about how quiet Polly was during the show. People often commented to Dalton and me about the children's good behavior in public and about how polite they were to adults. They had learned to answer, "Yes, Ma'am," and "No, Ma'am" to women and "Yes Sir," and "No, Sir" to men. It was a habit for them, and this was a source of pride for Dalton and for me.

Dalton and me
(holding Malinda)

Malinda Ruth

Allen Spencer

Mary Deanna

Rebecca Charlene

Polly Ann

Sarah Margaret

Dorothea Alicia

Me holding Alicia in
front of our house in
Brinker

THROUGH THE FIRE

In 1963 Dalton and I planned to take a little vacation. He had a few days off work, and we wanted to go West Texas and visit his mother, Stella Edwards, in Littlefield. I was packing our bags while the children darted in and out and bounced excitedly around the room. At that time we had four children ages eight and under: Malinda, Allen, Mary Deanna, and Becky. It would be a long drive for the children, but everyone was looking forward to seeing Grandmother. Our family lived simply and taking a road trip was a rare treat.

As Dalton loaded up the car, I set Allen's tricycle inside the house and locked the door to keep it safe. I checked everything twice and hoped I hadn't forgotten anything. At last we were on our way. Dalton and I listened to the radio as the kids played games in the back. They loved to play games with the cars we passed along the way. They would play "I Spy" for a while and then compete to see who could be the first to find all the letters in the alphabet on road signs and license plates. When they tired of that, they would burst into song. We didn't have a television at home, and the children had learned how to entertain themselves quite well. It was a noisy drive, but pleasant.

Three hundred miles later we arrived in Littlefield and made our way to Grandmother's house. She seemed very glad to see us, and met us at the door with hugs and kisses all around. The children were a little shy at first, because they hadn't been around her very often, but they soon warmed up to her and were off to explore the house. We had a nice visit with Stella, and she served us a huge Sunday dinner. We all stayed up late sharing stories until we grew sleepy. Finally we said, "Goodnight," and went to bed.

The long trip had its effect on the children and they were soon fast asleep. Our hearts were full. My husband worked Monday through Friday, every week of the year, except for his two weeks of vacation. It was so nice to finally relax and enjoy some time together. Dalton and I made our way to the guest room and within minutes, we were sleeping soundly. We were oblivious to the passage of time, but suddenly, there came the shrill ring of a telephone from the vicinity of the living room. Stella answered it and, after a moment, slipped into our room. She quietly said, "Son, it's for you."

"Now who could be calling us this time of night?" I wondered. Dalton, in a sleepy voice answered, "Hello." He listened for a few minutes with a serious expression on his face. He asked a couple of questions, and I watched his face anxiously, trying to read his thoughts. Then he hung up and looked directly at me. He paused for a moment, and then said, "That was Brother Alexander. Early this morning, our house burned to the ground. Nothing was saved. He said for us to stay here as long as we had originally planned and not to cut our vacation short. He said he would try to find us something."

We were stunned. Our house and all we owned, besides our car and what clothes we had with us, were gone. I once heard a lady in church who had lost her house in a fire say, "The Lord giveth and the Lord taketh away." I didn't know if I could say that then, but now I do. I just looked to God and trusted Him, and he gave me such peace. I thought about how we had our lives, and we had each other. We were so blessed to be out of harm's way when disaster struck. God can truly comfort us in times of trouble.

After spending a few days with Grandmother, we drove on to Midland where Dalton's sister, Alice, lived. She was very sympathetic of our situation and said, "Just be glad no one was hurt." She gave me a pretty dress that fit well and promised to send us a washing machine. She gave us a few household items as well.

All too quickly, our vacation was drawing to a close, and we started back to Commerce, not knowing what to expect. My folks lived in Bonham, so I said, "Honey, do you think we need to go by Mama's and stay there until you find out what Brother Alexander has found?" He said, "No, Brother Alexander said to meet him where the house used to be."

When we finally arrived, Brother and Sister Alexander were there. We stared at the place where the house had once stood. It was difficult to take it all in. After we had looked at the remains and cried a little, Brother Alexander said, "We found a place for you. Follow me." We followed he and his wife to a government housing project known as Durham Homes. They led us to one of the many duplexes, and we could hardly believe what we saw. There were four bedrooms, a kitchen, living room, bathroom and a pantry, far more than we could have imagined. As if that were not enough, the pantry was full of food. The refrigerator was stocked, and dinner was on the table! An apron was hanging on a hook, dishes and cookware were in the cabinets, and linens were in the closet. The bedrooms were all furnished and everything matched. The living room was also furnished and several of the church people were there to meet us. Our eyes were full of tears as we thanked them.

I had so many mixed emotions – love for them and love for God. This was truly better than anything we had had before. They said they'd had "lots of fun" going all over town gathering up furniture, food, clothes, dishes and linens that people donated. A lot of the furniture in the house was antique, especially the bedroom suite in Allen's room. There were large, old platters and other kitchen items, more than we would probably ever use. And people kept bringing clothes. People from the church and local community would show up at our door with more clothes to donate. Some didn't fit, but we appreciated each and every gesture of kindness. God only knows how grateful we were to have a place to come home to and for the love the church and community showed us; we never forgot. (Brother Alexander told us later that the reason they were able to get the duplex so quickly was because of Dalton's status as an Army veteran.)

As we went through the house, again, Allen looked around with a smile, but I noticed tears welling up in his eyes. He looked up at me and asked, "Mother, do tricycles burn?"

"Yes, honey, I'm afraid they do," I answered, remembering, ironically, how I had placed the tricycle inside the house to keep it safe.

The main thing I missed were my photographs. Losing your house in a fire is almost like a death. I had a camera with film in it that hadn't been developed. Somehow, I forgot to put it in the car for our trip, so it was destroyed. One day, however, Dalton went over to the burned house to look around. He came home later that day with a few pictures that were brown around the edges, and my Bible. He was holding it behind his back and asked mysteriously, "What can destroy the Word of God?" Then he showed me the Bible. It had some scorched places at the top, near the middle, on some pages, but was otherwise in good shape. I was so glad it was saved, and I was grateful for the photographs as well.

We still don't know for sure what started the fire. It was an old house with old plumbing and wiring. The tank in the bathroom was on the wall, and you pulled a chain to flush the toilet like the one the Olsons had in *Little House on the Prairie*. Some said the cause of the fire was probably a short in the electrical wiring. Then there was the possibility that the fire had been set intentionally; it seemed the landlord had a few enemies. But I hope it was just an accident, and I choose to think of it that way.

I am so thankful that we were not there when the house burned. I feel certain that had we been there, we would have all died that night. Allen's bed was back in the hall where they said the fire started. I just thank God that He allowed us to be far away when the fire occurred. And I am very grateful to our church family who was there for us in our time of need. They truly manifested a spirit of love and fulfilled Christ's teachings to the early church to "love one another."

Dalton and me in front of our house at Durham Homes in Commerce

Rebecca (left) and Mary Deanna at Durham Homes

ATTACHMENTS

One evening, when we still lived on Caddo Street in Commerce, a unique experience occurred. I was feeling pretty lonely at the time. I had four children under the age of seven, and Dalton was gone all evening. I had so many responsibilities, and I felt tired all the time. One night the wind was blowing hard, and there was snow on the ground. I was in the living room watching the kids play when Malinda thought she heard a dog barking outside. I tried to tell her it was just the wind, but she ran and opened the front door anyway. A little black dog dashed inside and hopped right up in my lap. I had never seen the dog before, but he seemed to know me. The weather was too bad to send him back outside, so I fed him and gave him some water. He stayed right by my side, and whenever I sat down again, he hopped right back up in my lap.

He was so sweet, and I loved him instantly.

The next day, when Dalton was home, we set out to look for the owner of the dog, but we never found who he belonged to. Dalton said he was a border collie, and I named him Blackie. Dalton had hunting dogs that he kept outside, but Blackie was mine. He lived inside with us, and I had a strong connection with him. Blackie seemed to know what I was thinking and understand how I was feeling. He brought me a lot of comfort.

Blackie was also protective of the kids. One day a man stopped by the house to try to sell us something. He reached out and put his hand on Allen's shoulder, and Blackie growled at him. The man took his hand away instantly and said, "That's okay; he's just watching out for the boy." I had never seen such a smart animal before.

When we moved to Durham Homes, after the fire, our new property manager, Mr. Kizer, was not fond of Blackie. He thought he was too aggressive and said he was afraid Blackie might bite someone. I really think he just didn't want any pets in the house. After that, though, Dalton took Blackie to his hunting buddy's (Mr. Tucker's) house, and he lived there for about two years. I missed him terribly. Then, when the family moved to Brinker, Dalton brought his hunting dogs with us, and Blackie came too. I was so thrilled to have him back, and our lease had nine acres of land that he could roam around on. I imagined how happy he would be romping through the grass and exploring every tree, creek, and rock.

Not long after we had settled in at Brinker, Blackie disappeared one day. I wasn't too concerned, because I figured he was probably wandering around the pasture. He stayed gone for a good while, and then I started to get worried. When he came back, I could tell right away that something was wrong. I was sitting on the front porch waiting for him. He came right up to me and gazed at me with the saddest look in his eyes. He looked like he was trying to tell me something, but I couldn't figure out what was wrong. Later that day, Dalton found him dead. He had been shot. I believe Blackie was trying to tell me goodbye.

Dalton laid the blame for Blackie's death on our neighbor to the east. He was a very unfriendly man, and probably wanted to teach us a lesson about keeping our animals off of his property. We never had any proof, but at other times, when our hunting dogs got loose, that neighbor would threaten to shoot them. I missed Blackie so much, and I never had another companion like him.

COMMUNITY AND COONHUNTING

We lived in the house at Durham Homes for four years. During that time, Polly and Sarah were born, just fifteen months apart. We had lots of neighbors, and the kids made friends with many of them. There were some widow ladies in the community who were especially nice to the children. Mrs. Fortenberry always had a kind word for them and would sometimes give them treats. Mrs. Carver was another one who loved to bake. She seemed to always have something fresh baked on hand, and she would offer the kids a cookie, or a piece of cake. She often invited Allen and Malinda to come to her house and watch television. She seemed to enjoy having them around. On Halloween, the kids would get dressed up and canvass the neighborhood, knocking on doors and collecting goodies. Mrs.

Carver was sure to give our kids homemade cookies or popcorn balls. The kids loved it. It was about the only time they got sweets at our house, except for ice cream or the occasional birthday cake.

The family that shared our duplex had almost as many kids as we did, but their oldest son had a mean streak. He would chase our kids and scare them. One time he got mad at Malinda about something and chased after her with a butcher knife. Their father had abandoned them, and the mom was trying to raise all of those children on her own. She eventually remarried, and her new husband adopted all of her children, and they moved out. The family that moved in after them had two sons named Guy and Roy who were close to Allen's age. They were very nice and polite.

A police officer lived behind our unit, and he had twin daughters who were about Polly's age. They would toddle over and sit on our back porch in their diapers and play. It seems like they always had runny noses, and one time they had impetigo, a highly contagious skin disease that causes oozing sores, especially around the mouth. I was so worried that Polly would get it, but she didn't.

One time Allen got a bad case of

ringworm (a kind of fungus) on his scalp and around his eyes. His eyes became sensitive to light. I guess he picked up the fungus from playing with a stray cat or from some other kids. I shaved his hair really short and covered all the sores with iodine every day until it cleared up. I had to get some drops for his eyes, and I kept him in a room with the lights off during the day. That was really hard on him, having to stay inside and not getting to play with other kids.

In 1966, Dalton left his job at American Wood and took a position on the evening shift at Rockwell International in Sulphur Springs. We rented a run-down house about seven miles outside of Sulphur Springs in a community called Brinker. The house in the projects seemed like a palace compared to this one. It was in the middle of a nine-acre cow pasture and had a cistern for water (with no filter) and a butane tank for cooking. There was no air conditioning (not even window units) and only a couple of gas space heaters for warmth. Our closest neighbors were T.H. and Vonda Burks, who lived about a quarter of a mile west of us. Between our house and theirs was a dairy barn.

I felt pretty isolated, and we had no way of

getting to services on weeknights when Dalton was working. Allen and Malinda were not old enough to drive, and I had never been issued a driver's license. I tried to learn a few times, but driving always made me very nervous. Since Dalton worked afternoons and evenings, we were without transportation most of the time. Brother Alexander often drove from Commerce to Brinker to pick us up for revival services. That was more than fifty miles, round trip, and he would have to do it twice each evening. It was a sacrifice on his part, but he was so sweet about it. He never seemed to mind; he just seemed happy to have us in church. Sometimes other people from the church would help as well. One time the drummer, Larry Yeager, who was also a university student, came and picked us up. He didn't know the way very well, and he took the longest route, which took about ten minutes longer each way. It never occurred to him to ask the kids the quickest way to the church. They knew all the shortcuts, but they were too polite to correct an adult.

When we first moved from Commerce, we had six children in the family, and Sarah was the baby. After we had lived at Brinker for about a year, I became pregnant again. We waited until it was almost time for me to deliver before we told the kids. It was December, and we told them they would be getting a new baby brother or sister for Christmas. Everyone was surprised and happy to learn that there would be a new baby in the family. Dorothea Alicia was born on December 16, 1967. We named her Dorothea after Dalton's sister, Jerry (whose given name was Dorothy Jo) and my sister, Dorothy Faye, and we named her Alicia, after Dalton's oldest sister, Trentie Alice.

With seven children, we had to find even more ways to make ends meet. On Saturday night, the children would all take baths and wash their hair. After it dried, the girls and I would all roll our hair for church on Sunday. We didn't have real rollers, so we would tear strips of paper from brown grocery sacks and fold them longways to make "curlers." I showed them how to twist their hair around the strips of paper, roll them up, and then tie the ends together. Sometimes a few of the curlers would come down during the night, but, overall, the plan worked, and the girls had curls for Sunday morning. Sometimes I would have a few sponge rollers that someone had given us, and I would leave my hair up until we got into the car. On the way to church, I would take them down and style my hair, so it would stay looking nice for the service.

To look at Sarah now, you would never know that at one time her hair was very thin and fine. When she was little, I would twist her hair into little rolls and hold it down with bobby pins. That's how I rolled her hair, and she'd have about three little curls. I always thought it was so cute! Well, in a catalogue Mary Deanna saw this long wig the same color as Sarah's strawberry blonde hair and thought it was so pretty. She wanted to order it for Sarah, and she finally convinced me. When it came in, Sarah wore it to church, and it came down nearly to her waist. I'm telling you, that was the happiest kid you ever saw.

As I have mentioned, Mary Deanna was born with strabismus, and she wore corrective lenses from a very early age. Everyone thought she was so cute with her little glasses, but her eyes caused her to have some difficulties in school. Her glasses were very thick, and she still had trouble focusing. We took her to a specialist, and he recommended that Mary Deanna do exercises to strengthen her eyes. One of the things they told us to do was to let her jump on a trampoline. The university had some great big indoor trampolines, so sometimes the four oldest kids would walk down there and jump. They really enjoyed that, and they got pretty good at developing their balance. The doctor also recommended that Mary attend Head Start, which was a program that had recently begun in Commerce. We enrolled her and she went there for a year, and then she went to first grade. When we moved to Sulphur Springs, though, they wanted to hold her back a year. That was so hard on Mary Deanna. She was a smart girl, and it was frustrating for her that she couldn't see properly. When she was in third grade, we were able to have surgery done on her eyes to have them straightened. The surgery was successful, and she was able to wear regular glasses (for farsightedness). She was another happy kid, and she was so proud to have her school photo taken that year without any corrective lenses.

In 1972, we got tired of making the long drive to Commerce every Sunday morning and Sunday night, so we decided to leave Commerce First Assembly and begin attending the First Assembly of God Church in Sulphur Springs. Besides, I had always admired Sister Patsy Ruth Allen, and she was the pastor's wife. She had been a role model for me when I was just nineteen years old, and she was a big influence in my life. Her husband was Reverend Cletus Allen, and they had a daughter named Cleta Ruth. I was the main one who wanted to change churches, but it was difficult for us to make the adjustment, especially since the Alexanders felt like family. The kids adjusted pretty easily, but they missed their friends. They really didn't understand why we were changing.

The people at the Sulphur Springs church welcomed our family, but they did not embrace Dalton the way Brother Alexander had. In Commerce, he had been one of the church leaders, but he never had an important role in Sulphur Springs because he had been married before. The Allens were very conservative and did not allow anyone who was remarried to hold an office in the church. Business meetings were held at the church once a year, and sometimes Dalton would be nominated by one of the members for the office of deacon. Brother Allen would read the requirements for the office from 1 Timothy 3: 8-13, which included the phrase, "Let deacons each be the husband of one wife," and then he would take a vote. All of our kids voted for their dad out of loyalty. When Brother Allen counted the votes,

Dalton would have the lead. Then, Dalton would stand up and ask them to count again, and he would instruct his seven children not to raise their hands. When they counted the second time, he never had enough votes to take office. I think that was a blow to his ego. Having graduated with a four-year degree from Southwestern Bible College, he was more qualified (on paper) than anyone in the church, except for the pastor. He began to change, slowly, over time. Without the respect of the pastor or the support of the congregation, he was not as strict as he used to be. He used to never entertain hunting buddies on Sunday, but in Sulphur Springs, he starting letting Marshall Hopper come over every Sunday afternoon, and he would stay practically the entire day. It seemed like we never had any family time.

One of Dalton's hobbies was breeding and raising purebred dogs. He started off with greyhounds, but the buyers were racing them and gambling on them. He (or perhaps the church) didn't approve of that, so he wound up selling the greyhounds and getting out of that side business. He still had a hobby, though; he loved to hunt raccoons, or coon hunt, as it is called in East Texas. One of his good hunting buddies was Dr. Floyd R. Vest, a math professor at East Texas State University, which later became Texas A&M University - Commerce. Dr. Vest and his wife, Wyona lived in Commerce and attended First Assembly of God Church. Floyd became the Sunday School teacher, and he told the class, "I just think people ought to put their feet under each other's table more often." Dalton said, "Well, if you can stand it, come on over." We all got to talking, and I was thinking to myself, "I could never be friends with them." They seemed reserved and perhaps in a different social class. After a while, though, as we all got to know one another, I realized that the Vests were very friendly, especially Wyona. She was warm and talkative, and really made me feel at home. And she was very thoughtful; she would find ways to help us without making it feel like charity, like passing her girls' dresses down to our younger children.

Floyd was several years younger than Dalton, but they seemed to enjoy each other's company. Pretty soon, we started inviting the Vests over, and they invited our family over to their place. Floyd would come to the house and go all through it; he would act like he was completely at home. If there was any food on the table, he would just reach out and get some. One time I had some hotdogs on the table, and he just went in there and started eating them. He didn't seem to think anything about it. He really took the phrase literally, "Make yourself at home."

One time the Vests went to Missouri for two weeks during the winter, and they offered to let our family stay in their house while they were gone. They didn't like the idea of us being out there at Bottom's Place, because it was so cold. We had three children at that time under the age of six, and Mary Deanna was just a baby. She was about the same age as their first daughter, Martha. We packed up our things and moved into their house. Their home was much nicer than ours, and I worked so hard to keep everything clean. The only mishap was that Mary Deanna did something to their clock. It was an old clock and one of Floyd's prized possessions. He was crazy about that clock. Dalton gave him some money to get the clock fixed, and we replaced the groceries that we used, but I felt very bad about the accident. When the Vests came home, they all got sick. I don't know if they took a virus on the way home, or what.

Later on, Dr. Vest took a position at the University of North Texas, and they moved to

Denton. Floyd would still come back periodically to go coon hunting and spend the night with our family. Malinda's room served as the guest room if we had company. One evening, Floyd came over, and he brought another man with him. We didn't have any extra room, so those poor guys had to share a bed. I changed the sheets and sprayed some perfume in the bed and in the air, so it would smell nice. That night I heard those men start sneezing. Just about the time things would get quiet, we'd hear them sneezing again. I had a pretty good laugh about that.

That was actually the kind of stunt Floyd Vest would appreciate, because he had a very dry sense of humor. One time he went to a dog show with Dalton and Allen. Vendors would often come by and hand out free samples of their products to the spectators. Someone came by passing out sample packages of dry dog food. With a face just as straight as could be, Floyd opened up that package and started eating the dog food just like it was a bag of peanuts. People must have looked at him like he was out of his mind. Allen thought that was so funny, and he told that story again and again.

When the family moved to Brinker, Floyd

came and stayed over a couple of days and built a workroom outside for Dalton. He had to start from the ground up, so it was a very big commitment. Dalton was working, so Floyd pretty much had to do it by himself. He would get busy working, and his britches would drop way down in the back. The kids would watch him through the window, and they thought that was pretty funny. He wanted one of the girls to come out and help him take measurements. I sent Becky out there, and she worked with him for a while. He talked to her and asked her questions. About all she did was hold the tape measure and read off numbers for him.

With Dalton working nights, it might have seemed odd to outsiders to have Dr. Vest there in the house, but he was like one of the family. He was always willing to help anyone who needed it, and even now, in his eighties, he still works with a men's group at his church to repair houses for people in need.

Another hunting buddy of Dalton's was Marshall Hopper. Dalton met him when we moved to Brinker, and everyone just called him Marshall. He and Dalton often went to dog shows together and to "hunting nights" that were typically held on the weekend. These were competition hunts, and dogs could win trophies and earn a name for themselves, making them worth a good deal of money. The owners would show the dogs during the day and hunt them at night. Dalton had anywhere from ten to twenty hunting dogs at any given time, and we had shelves full of trophies. Once, when two of the dogs had a litter of puppies about the same time, the kids counted thirty dogs on our property. It's a wonder that we could feed them all. One time, Dalton sold his registered grand champion hunting and show dog, Sonny Boy, for $2,000 (which would be the equivalent of about $12,000 today). That money could have really helped our family, but Dalton could not bear to be without Sonny. He wound up buying him back for $1,000, plus another dog. The kids and I were really disappointed about that.

The championship hunts and dog shows usually occurred on Saturdays and took up the entire day; then Marshall would come over on Sunday to discuss the hunt. He usually showed up right when the family was eating lunch, but he never would eat with us. He and Dalton loved discussing the dogs, the hunt, and reading what the coon hunting magazines had to say. Then around 6:00pm, we would all get ready and go back to church. This schedule didn't give Dalton much time to rest from his 3:00pm to midnight job, and it certainly didn't give him much time with the kids or with me. I never understood why he let Marshall come over on Sundays. When we were in Commerce, he had a very strict rule that he would not entertain on Sundays unless the guest was going to church with us. If someone came to the house to visit, they attended service with us that evening, but Marshall never did.

Another hunting buddy Dalton got to know and become very fond of was Thorowgood Taylor Brown III, born on July 18, 1945 to Thorowgood Taylor J. Brown and Dorothy Bell Brown. We called him T. Taylor Brown for short or just Taylor. He was only about seventeen when we met him, but he was very interested in coon hunting. His grandpa gave him permission to hunt with Dalton. Taylor became a regular visitor to our house and was sort of like an older brother or uncle to the kids. He was ten years older than Malinda, our oldest, so he related to the kids very well. Sometimes he would go outside and play with them and chase them all around the house. He was full of energy. The kids looked forward to his visits, and Allen, especially, looked up to him. Allen often joined Dalton and Taylor on their hunting ventures. Dalton first met Taylor when our family lived on Caddo Street in Commerce, before the house burned, but he kept coming to visit and hunt, even after we moved to Brinker.

When Taylor was a young man (about twenty-two or twenty-three) he and Dalton went hunting on a very cold night. The roads were slippery, and some of the trees had ice on them. They shouldn't have even been out there. Well, the dogs treed a coon, and Taylor wanted to climb the tree to get the coon down. Dalton told him not to climb it, but Taylor did anyway. Taylor made it up into the branches and was trying to scare the coon and make him jump. The limbs were very slippery, and Taylor lost his grip and fell to the ground. It was awful. Taylor was lying there hurt, but Dalton didn't want to carry him back to the truck for fear of hurting him worse. Dalton had to leave him lying on the ground, hike back to the truck, and rush home to call an ambulance. Dalton was very upset when he got to the house. It may be the most affected I had ever seen him. His face was white, and his jaw was rigid. He made the call, and then rushed back to be with Taylor. The ambulance came and took Taylor to the hospital. His leg was badly broken, and it took him a long time to recover. As a result of his injuries, Taylor ended up having to wear an elevated shoe on one foot. When we saw him again, he was very changed. Gone was the quick-moving young man so full of energy and life. He moved more slowly, and one shoe had a very thick sole. It seemed to take more effort for him to walk. I have always regretted that incident and would give anything if I could have talked them out of going that night.

Taylor still liked Dalton, and hunting after that, but he stayed away for a while and went to college. I can only imagine what his grandparents thought of us. One day he came to visit and brought presents for everyone. I think that was his way of letting us know that he didn't hold a grudge. A few years later, Taylor married a sweet girl named Cathy Lee Head. They moved to Cypress, Texas (near Houston) and had a son, whom they named Thorowgood Taylor Brown IV. We didn't hear from him anymore after that. Years later, when Allen was married and had children, he named his youngest son Taylor after T. Taylor Brown III.

Allen, Malinda, Becky, Mary, Polly, and Sarah at Durham Homes

Alicia (left) and Sarah standing near one of Dalton's hunting dogs

(L to R) Polly, Sarah, Alicia, and Becky all dressed up for a visit from Taylor Brown (Polly and Alicia are holding puppies.

The house we rented in Brinker

GETTING BY

We were very crowded at the house in Brinker. Dalton and I had our private bedroom, and Allen, being the only boy had his own room at the back of the house, next to the bathroom. Allen was very particular and kept his room neat and organized. He would get very upset if anyone messed with his toys or moved books or other items out of place. The girls all shared the other bedroom. Malinda had a half-bed to herself on one side of the room, while Mary Deanna, Becky, Polly, and Sarah slept crossways on a full bed. Alicia slept in a crib in the living room, next to our bedroom. Malinda was older and needed more privacy, but we just didn't have the space. She didn't like having to share with all the little girls, and there were frequent arguments.

At the back of the house was an addition that we called "the storage room." The landlord's wife, Mrs. Burks, had a hobby of making dolls, and she had filled that little room with all of her supplies. There were piles and boxes full of net and fabric, doll heads, and bodies. I tried to keep the kids out of her things, but it was hard. They liked to go in there and explore. I guess she figured out what was happening, because, finally, one day she came and got all of her stuff and hauled it off to another location. That room had big cracks around the door, no insulation, and the wind blew straight through at night, so we thought we would store some things out there. Dalton brought in the two fifty-pound bags of dog food that he always kept on hand, and we had some tools in there as well, hanging on the wall. The door that went outside from that room, just had a hook and eye latch on it, and it did very little to keep out the elements. But low and behold, Mary Deanna and Becky got it into their heads that they wanted to move into the storage room and make it their bedroom. I wasn't too sure about that, but I talked it over with Dalton, and we decided to let them do it. By then, Mary Deanna was about ten years old, and Becky was eight.

They worked on getting that room all cleaned up, and Dorothy Faye gave us a set of bunkbeds to put in there. The girls put the beds side by side, and they were almost touching. There was just room enough for them to squeeze between the beds to get in. We also had an old chest of drawers someone had given us, and that is all the furniture they had. We didn't have enough blankets and quilts for the extra beds, and there wasn't a heater out there, so in the winter, Mary Deanna and Becky would pile layers of clothes on top of their sheets to keep them warm. At night, they could hear mice crunching on the dog food. If they had to go to the bathroom during the night, they had to walk past the dog food (and rodents), through Allen's room, and into the bathroom. It was barely a step above camping, but the girls were willing to do it in order to have their own room.

We only had the one toilet for nine people, but there was an old outhouse out back that could be used if someone really needed to go. The outhouse also came in handy when the plumbing was backed up, and that happened pretty often. The kids didn't like the outhouse because it stank badly, and there were weeds grown up all around it. Inside, there was a wide wooden plank with a big hole cut out in the middle. There were usually flies buzzing around in there, not speak of wasps and yellow jackets and other insects that built nests in and around the structure. The whole thing looked like it would fall over in a high wind, but amazingly, it never did. We got more use out of that old outhouse than I like to admit.

In the winter, it was too cold to make the kids go outside during the night, so if we had plumbing problems, they would have to use a pot. This was a chamberpot with a lid. They would do their business, and then put the lid back on to contain the odor. In the morning, I would have to carry the pot outside and empty it. We didn't have to resort to that too often, but there were times when we were glad to have it.

Another thing we ran low on very often was toilet tissue. We just never seemed to buy enough on our weekly trips to the grocery store. Having grown up during the Depression, I knew a thing or two about making do during shortages. We would take old newspapers and rub them between our hands to soften them up and use that for toilet paper. If we didn't have newspaper, we used paper grocery bags, which I saved for just such an occasion, and there was always the Sears and Roebuck catalogue as a last resort. Somehow, we always managed to figure something out until

Dalton could make it back to the grocery store on Friday.

Our children had it pretty rough compared to most of their friends, but there were good times too. The kids loved for me to tell them stories, and I guess, in a way, I have been telling stories all my life. All those years in Sunday School, telling stories to my imaginary friends, served me well, because the thing the kids liked to hear most of all was Bible stories. When Dalton was at work, they would come into my room and pile into bed with me. I would tell them about Joseph and his coat of many colors, about Moses leading the Hebrew children out of the land of Egypt, about Daniel in the lion's den, about David and Goliath, about Queen Esther and the wicked Haman, about Sampson and Delilah, about Ruth and Boaz, and Jacob and Esau. The kids would usually request the story they wanted to hear, and I would tell them in depth, going back over all the details from the Bible that were imprinted on my mind and making sure to teach them a lesson with each one. Sometimes they requested other stories, like the *Country Mouse and the City Mouse*, or *Peter Rabbit*. They especially loved to hear stories about themselves. They would say, "Tell me what I did when I was a little girl." I would try to remember all the cute little things they did and tell them in a way that made them feel special. Lying there in the bed after a long day, I would start to get sleepy and sometimes fall asleep in the middle of the story. The kids wouldn't let me get by with that. They always wanted to hear how the story ended, even though they knew them all by heart.

Things were pretty peaceful when the kids were home from school. They were usually doing homework or outside playing. Occasionally they would get into squabbles, and I would have to step in. But when the weather was bad, they had to play inside, and then things could get pretty rowdy, especially if they started having pillow fights. The girls liked to play house and dolls, and they also liked to hold church services. One of the girls, usually Polly, would preach, and the rest, with their dolls, would be the congregation. After the preaching, they would all go down to the altar and pray, and they really seemed to get a blessing. Allen would usually go to his room and read or draw. He was a good artist. All of the kids can draw, but Allen really seemed to take an interest in it. Malinda also had a talent for drawing, but more than anything, she loved to read. She almost always had a book going. All the kids could entertain themselves for hours, reading, drawing, making paper dolls, sewing, or making up games.

One evening when Dalton was at work, the sky became very brassy looking and I just knew a storm was coming. Our flimsy house was in the middle of a pasture with seven big oak trees strewn out over several acres and a few random cows grazing here and there. As I prepared dinner for the kids, I kept watching the sky and wondering what was going to happen. About the time we sat down to eat, rain began to pelt the house. The roof was severely damaged, so we were used to having water leaking into the house in several places. The kids grabbed buckets and pans and put them around the house to catch the rain and keep water off the floor; then we all sat down around the long table that was positioned at one end of the living room, near the kitchen. We said grace and began eating, and I tried to keep the kids' minds off the storm by talking about their day.

Pretty soon, lightening was flashing all around and thunder was cracking so loudly, that the house vibrated. Allen was sitting at the foot of the table with his back to the window, and the other kids sat on the sides, with me at the head. We didn't have any curtains or blinds, so the windows were bare and made it hard to ignore what was happening outside. Suddenly, the wind picked up, and the house shook so hard that I just knew something was about to give. I told the kids to leave their plates and move to the kitchen. They all got up quickly, except Allen; he really hated to leave his food behind. But with a little urging from me, he finally left his plate and pushed his chair in. Just as he came around the corner of the table to enter the kitchen, a gust of wind smashed into the window, and glass shattered all across the table. We stared at it in shock. If it had happened just seconds earlier, we might have all been seriously injured, and especially Allen. The kids all huddled around me in the kitchen, and we gave thanks to God for sparing our lives and asked him to let the storm pass quickly and to keep other people safe as well.

When the thunder began to move away and the rain became lighter, we all went back into the living room to assess the damage. Shards of glass lay all over the table and on the floor. We carefully picked up the glass and soaked up as much water as we could. Then I swept the floor and told all the kids not to walk in there barefoot until we could clean it better. I found an old sheet to put across the window, and gave thanks again, that no one was hurt.

The next morning, we found that two of our cows had huddled underneath a tree for protection from the rain and had been struck by lightening. They both lay dead on the ground. Even though it had been several hours, and their bodies were looking distended, Dalton loaded the carcasses and took them into town to have them butchered. Our freezer had never been so full, and the children, and hunting dogs, ate very well for quite some time. It's a wonder we didn't all get sick, but no one did.

MISSION TRIP

When we were at the church in Commerce, there was a man named Bill Dickey who had been in trouble for stealing a car, and he spent some time in the pen. He was also a heavy drinker. He starting coming to church regularly and got saved. There was also a missionary from our church named Katie Jean Jones, who was single. Ever so often, she would speak to the congregation about her mission work and raise money to help sponsor her for the next year. Well, she and Bill Dickey met each other and fell in love. They moved to Kentucky, and together, they devoted their lives to an organization called Teen Challenge, which offers help to young men who have been in trouble.

As I mentioned earlier, we moved the family to Sulphur Springs and eventually changed our membership to the church there. One day, the pastors, Cletus and Patsy Ruth Allen, invited the Dickeys to speak to our congregation. Of course Bill and Katie Jean knew our family from the Commerce congregation, and they wanted Malinda to go back with them and work as a volunteer at Teen Challenge. At first, she wanted to go, and everyone was excited for her. The church even gave her a going away shower to help with some of the items she would need for the summer. Everything was ready, and then she met a young man named Leonardo Elias. She decided not to go with Katie Jean and Bill after all. The pastor came all the way to the house to get Malinda, but she wanted to stay in Texas and get married instead.

Mary Deanna understood what was happening, and she felt that someone should go in Malinda's place, especially since a commitment had already been made, but Mary wasn't quite old enough. She was only fifteen, and the rule was that volunteers had to be at least sixteen. Sister Allen talked to the Dickeys, and they decided to give Mary a chance. Mary Deanna traveled to Louisville, Kentucky with them where she would spend the entire summer taking care of their children, cleaning the house, and helping with anything else they needed. Katie Jean had very high standards, and Mary worked hard to please her. She had very little free time but Mary would sometimes go walking around a little pond in the evening for some quiet time.

Mary Deanna said later that she was actually too young to be away from home, and that she should not have gone. She learned a lot, though, and the experience did shape and change her. If people would get into an argument at home, Mary would say, "There is a better way." She had learned about conflict resolution by being with the Dickeys and seeing how they counseled the young men at Teen Challenge.

While Mary Deanna was at Teen Challenge, the family moved to a house in Tyre, Texas, about thirty minutes from where we had lived before. Dalton had been saving some money, and with the help of a V.A. loan, bought a few acres of land, and an old frame house that he had moved onto the property. The kids told Mary about the move, and she was so excited to come home. She was used to living in nicer surroundings with the Dickeys and was not looking forward to going back to the house we had been living in when she left. (It was in Dike, TX and was used by the owners as a hay barn until we decided to rent it.)

When Mary flew into Dallas, Dalton and some of the kids picked her up at the airport. That was the first time any of them had ever been to an airport or anywhere near a plane. When Mary Deanna came home and saw the house, all of her excitement disappeared. She was so disappointed she started to cry. And even though it was better then Brinker or Dike, it was in pretty bad shape. After being moved, the house needed to leveled, but Dalton never got around to having that done. Someone once said that every room in the house slanted off in a different direction, and he was about right. None of the doors would shut properly. One thing that helped Mary Deanna feel a little better was that a shipment of clothes had recently arrived from West Texas, and many of the items fit her perfectly. She had grown some over the summer, and the beautiful dresses that her cousins sent fit her to a tee. She was able to start the new school year, at a new school, in style.

Mary as a teenager

STORYTELLING

When Allen was about fourteen, he started working for T.H. Burks. Allen was already good friends with T.H.'s sons, Roger and Gary, and they had been our closest neighbors for years. T.H.'s dad owned most of the land, so Allen was really working for him. Allen would milk the cows, haul hay, mend fences, or whatever needed to be done. He was a hard worker, and he saved his money. When he turned sixteen, Allen got his driver's license and bought his first car with his own money. It was the first time we had ever had a driver in the family in the evenings. With Dalton's work schedule, we had always depended on other people to give us a ride. Many young guys would have wanted a snazzy-looking sports car, but Allen, very pragmatically, thought of the size of our family, and bought a station wagon. It was so nice to be able to go to revivals at church without having to ask for help from other people. We were also able to go visit my parents and Lena May in Sherman more often.

Allen went to college at East Texas State University for a semester or two, where he planned to study art, but then he got a job working at Kroger. Later, he traded in the station wagon and bought a sharp-looking 1973 Ford Mustang. He was very proud of that car. Sometimes he would give the kids a ride to school. They had always ridden the bus, so it was pretty nice to be dropped off in front of the school in such a nice car.

When Malinda was nineteen, she married a man who had immigrated to the United States from Mexico. We didn't know much about him, but he was very nice and seemed to be crazy about Malinda. Malinda became pregnant, and about three months later, her husband, Leonardo, had to leave for Mexico but promised to return quickly. He was gone for months, and Malinda began to lose hope that he would ever return. Finally, one day, he called and spoke to Dalton on the phone. He said that he had been stopped at the border, and he didn't know when he could make it back, but he promised to keep trying. Malinda was furious and began to seek a divorce. She learned that Leonardo already had a wife and two children in Mexico, so she was able to have the marriage annulled. When her baby was born, she named her Jodee Maria. (The "dee" was after Dalton's middle name, Dee, and Maria was for me, Mary).

Malinda wasn't ready to live on her own and be a mother, so she asked me to raise her daughter, and I became Jodee's legal guardian. She was like my own daughter and was just ten years younger than Alicia. She was a great comfort to me when all the kids were grown and left home. I had always hated the thought of ever being alone, and with Jodee in the house, I didn't have to be. And besides, raising her gave me a purpose. When Jodee married, she had twin boys named Tyler and Trevor. Her marriage didn't last, and she moved back in with me. Now I was raising my great grandsons as well. It was difficult to keep up with them sometimes, but like my children and grandchildren, they loved to hear stories. I told them the usual Bible stories, but one day Tyler and Trevor asked me to tell them a story about a vacuum cleaner. They liked all kinds of appliances and enjoyed taking them apart to see how they worked. They were especially fascinated by the vacuum cleaner. Well, I didn't know any stories about vacuum cleaners, so I made up one for them. I called it *Bill, the Vacuum Cleaner*. The boys loved it, and that became their favorite story. They would ask to hear it over and over. Finally, one day, I decided to write it down.

Bill, the Vacuum Cleaner

Bill was a shiny, new vacuum cleaner. He had just been assembled in a factory and had been sent to Tom's Hardware Store for their annual Christmas sale. Many people would be shopping for vacuum cleaners this season, and Bill was hoping that a nice family would buy him and give him a new home. All the vacuum cleaners in Tom's store were lined up in a row, and Bill felt so excited to be there. At the factory, they had tested him to be sure he was well made. It was the first time he got to see what it was like to vacuum. He enjoyed it so much; he could hardly wait to vacuum again. After all, that is what he had been made for!

So now, the day before Christmas, he

was standing with the other vacuum cleaners, fairly bursting with excitement. Bill's little heart was beating fast and loud. As people came in and out of the hardware store, Bill watched the door and hoped that someone would come and buy him very soon.

Just then, a man wearing a suit and a hat came in the door. "Oh," thought Bill, "I hope he comes over here and buys me!" The man walked straight over to the vacuum cleaners. He took a quick look at Bill but kept on moving down the aisle. Bill's heart sank. The man was looking at the big, powerful vacuum cleaners. Bill thought to himself, "I can work just as hard as they can. I love to vacuum!"

Suddenly, the man turned around and came back to Bill. He looked him over closer this time. Bill was so excited! The man said to the clerk, "I'll take this one. It's a Christmas present for my wife. Please wrap it in pretty paper with a big red bow, and I want to add a card also." The man wrote on the card and placed Bill in the backseat of his car, and away they drove to his new home.

When they arrived, the man in the suit

placed his package under a lovely tree. Even though he was all wrapped up, Bill hardly slept a wink that night. He could hardly wait until morning.

Christmas morning, the family came rushing into the living room to open gifts. The man's wife saw a big present under the tree and thought to herself, "Oh, I hope this is a vacuum cleaner! I do need a new one, and the kids love to run the vacuum cleaner too." She eagerly opened the package as she read the card that said, "Dear Sue, I hope you and the children enjoy this special gift. From your loving husband, John. "

"Thank you so much!" exclaimed Sue. This is just what I wanted!" She smiled happily at her husband.

Bill, the vacuum cleaner, was so happy that his new owners were pleased with him. He was eager to show them what a good job he could do. After everyone had opened presents, eaten popcorn, and played with their toys, Sue decided this was a good time to try out her new gift.

Bill was jumping up and down inside. He was so excited to get to work. Sue plugged in the cord, and Bill's engine hummed to life. She vacuumed a small space around the

Christmas tree where the needles had fallen. Bill worked perfectly! He ran so quietly, and he picked up every tiny piece of debris on the floor. He didn't miss a thing. "Oh, John, I am so pleased with this gift!" Sue said, putting her arms around her husband. Sue gave John a kiss, and John smiled a happy smile. "Now I'm really going to see what he can do," Sue thought to herself. She took the vacuum cleaner into each room and vacuumed all around. Bill happily zipped into the corners. He quietly dashed under the beds. He found all the lint, and hair, and dust that had been mashed into the carpet. He found every crumb that had been dropped by the children. He even found a whisker that had fallen off of the cat. Sue's carpets had never been so clean or looked so good!

Bill was happier than he had ever been. He felt a wonderful feeling of accomplishment. He knew that he was where he was supposed to be and doing exactly what he was meant to do, and he was doing it to the best of his ability. He was completely satisfied. That night, he slept soundly and dreamed of his next opportunity to work with all of him might.

And so it is with us. God has a plan for each one of us. Proverbs 19:21 says, "You can make many plans, but God's purpose will prevail." (NLT). When we do what God has planned for us, we will be completely happy. He gives us the gifts and abilities to complete the job he has given us to do, and he wants us to do it with a good attitude. The more we read God's word and pray to him, the more God will show us his purpose for our lives.

Putting that story down on paper was very rewarding, and I began to get ideas for more stories. That urge I had to write back in high school never went away, and I hoped that one day I could get something published. I was already famous in my family for being a letter writer. I would write letters to senators, representatives, the president, preachers, doctors, company owners, and many other people. I always felt like I could express myself better in writing than on the phone or in person, and I was able to resolve a lot of problems that way. At church, I started writing cards to people who hadn't attended in a while. It was very rewarding to reach out to them and let them know we were thinking of them, and people really seemed to appreciate that.

Finally in 2018, I wrote down one of the stories from the Bible that I had always wanted to share. I wrote about Naomi, Ruth, and Boaz from the book of Ruth, and I added in some of the details that are not given in the Bible, like the food they may have eaten, what the characters were thinking and feeling, and tried to give a complete picture, while staying true to the biblical account. That story was published in 2020 under the title, *Naomi's Journey*[1]. My lifelong dream had finally become a reality.

[1] Philips, Mary. *Naomi's Journey*: 2020 (available on Amazon and as a Kindle ebook)

Allen with
his first car

Alicia, Jodee, and
Craig Connor
(Frank and
Dorothy's
youngest son)

SPREADING HOPE

Shortly after finishing the manuscript for *Naomi's Journey*, I started working on an essay about meekness, based on Galatians 5:22-23. I wanted to share my thoughts with other Christians in the hopes or providing inspiration to them. Below is the piece that I wrote.

Blessed are the Meek

Blessed are the meek for they shall inherit the earth (Matt 5:5, KJV).

The fruit of the Spirit proceeds naturally from a life that is lived in submission to the will of God. When an individual accepts Jesus Christ as their savior, the Holy Spirit enters that person's life. If they walk in the spirit daily, living in faith and obedience to God's word, eventually, the fruit of the Spirit will be as evident in their life as the fruit that grows on a tree.

Galations 5:22-23 teaches that there are nine manifestations of the spirit of God working in our lives, and one of those is meekness. Meekness can be compared with quietness and humility. A person who demonstrates meekness does not try to be seen or heard above others. They are selfless and tend to put the needs of others before their own needs. The meek in spirit are humble and trust in God to work out their problems; they do not become upset, worried, or fearful when trouble comes their way. They believe God's word and have confidence that God will keep his promises. And above all, they maintain inner peace even if God does not answer their prayers or come to their rescue right away. They are willing to submit to the will of God and wait patiently upon him.

One of the meekest men who ever lived

was Moses. God says he was the meekest man on Earth, and calls him a "friend" (Exodus 33:11 KJV). God called Moses to lead his people out of Egyptian bondage where they had been slaves for hundreds of years and had been praying for God to deliver them. Moses thought he was not properly equipped to be a leader for his people. He felt that he could not speak well enough, but through various signs, God convinced Moses that he would equip him for the job. Though there were many setbacks when Moses approached Pharaoh, and it looked as though Moses would not succeed, he placed his faith completely in God and trusted him to bring deliverance. Moses continued to obey God until at last he led the children of Israel out of Egypt. After that the Israelites gave Moses all kinds of problems. They murmured, complained, criticized, worshipped idols, and even asked to be taken back to Egypt. They accused Moses of bringing them out into the wilderness to let them die (Ex 14:11, KJV).

Through it all, Moses kept his faith in God, but one day he became angry with the ungrateful children of Israel. The people were hungry and needed water. God told Moses to speak to a rock and it would spring forth with fresh water. In his frustration with the people, Moses struck the rock with his staff rather than speaking to it. Because of this moment of weakness, God did not permit Moses to enter into the Promised Land of Canaan. Moses fervently prayed and asked God to change his mind, but God would not allow it (Deut 3: 23-25, KJV). Moses submitted to God's will and did not ask again. Because of his humility, and his many years of faithful service, God allowed Moses to view the Promised Land from the top of a high mountain, but he appointed a new leader, Joshua, to lead the Israelites into that land. Moses's time of service to God was over and God took him. Deuteronomy 34:7 tells us that "Moses was an hundred and twenty years old when he died: his eye was not dim, nor his natural force abated" (KJV). God blessed him abundantly and used him mightily to do the work of his kingdom.

Through Moses's example we see that submitting to the will of God and remaining humble and obedient keeps us in right relationship with him. When we allow pride and self-righteousness to get in the way, we drift further from God and lose sight of his plan for our lives. Even when the circumstances seem hopeless, we must understand that God is still in control and is moving on our behalf.

Another individual in the Bible who demonstrates meekness is Joseph. He was one of the twelve sons of Jacob and was his father's favorite. Jacob made Joseph a beautiful coat, and his brothers became jealous and were cruel to him. One day Joseph told his brothers of a dream he had had in which they all bowed down and worshipped him (Genesis 37:7-8). His brothers hated him and decided to kill him. One of his brothers, Rueben, convinced the others to throw Joseph into a dry cistern instead. He had plans to return him to his father when things settled down (Genesis 37:21). But when a caravan of Midianite traders passed through on their way to Egypt, the brothers sold Joseph into slavery.

Once Joseph reached Egypt, he became a servant to a man named Potiphar, who was one of Pharaoh's officials (Gen 37:21). Although Joseph was loyal and faithful, Potiphar's wife lied about him to her husband and falsely accused him of sexually assaulting her. Joseph was cast into prison for a crime he did not commit. Joseph maintained a meek and quiet spirit, and while he was in prison, God was still with him and blessed him. Joseph won favor with the head prison guard and finally there came an opportunity for Joseph to do what God had shown him in his dream.

Joseph interpreted dreams in prison for Pharaoh's wine taster and his baker, and unlike others who tried to give interpretations, Joseph's predictions came true. Later, when the wine taster was restored to his position, Pharaoh had a dream that none of his wise men could interpret. The wine taster then remembered Joseph and told Pharaoh about him. Joseph interpreted Pharaoh's dream and told him of a great famine that was coming upon the land. Then Pharaoh elevated Joseph to second in command over his entire kingdom. When the famine came, Joseph's brothers traveled to Egypt to buy grain. Joseph recognized them and was moved with compassion. Joseph was in a powerful position where he could have easily taken revenge upon his brothers, but he chose to remain humble before God and help them. After testing them in various ways, Joseph revealed himself to his brothers and forgave them. He told them, "But as for you, ye thought evil against me; but God meant it unto good, to bring to pass, as it is this day, to save much people alive" (Gen 50:20, KJV).

Through many trials and much pain

Joseph suffered, but God kept his word to him. Joseph's life demonstrates that when we are humble and faithful to God, he will elevate us and crown us with honor. Proverbs 22:4 states: "True humility and fear of the Lord lead to riches, honor, and long life" (NLT).

In the New Testament, Jesus provides the perfect example of meekness. Jesus says, "...I am meek and lowly in heart" (Matt 11: 29 KJV). Before Jesus began his ministry, he fasted forty days and nights in the wilderness, and then he was tempted by the devil three times. By resisting temptation, and quoting the word of God, Jesus caused the devil to flee. Jesus returned from the wilderness full of the Holy Spirit. Many people loved him and believed on him when they heard him teach; Jesus had great compassion on the multitudes of followers, and he healed and delivered them. The local scribes and Pharisees felt threatened by his ministry and did all they could to destroy him. For three and a half years Jesus was persecuted by the religious leaders while he went about doing good: healing the sick, raising the dead, and saving sinners. Finally, he was betrayed by Judas, one of his own disciples, falsely accused by the court, and denied by Peter, one of his own disciples. He was brutally whipped and condemned to be crucified on a cross. Even in death, Jesus showed mercy and compassion; he forgave a repentant thief who was dying on a cross next to him; he thought of his mother and asked John to care for her, and he asked God to forgive the people. He cried out from the cross, "Father forgive them for they know not what they do" (Luke 23: 34, KJV).

Everyone saw Jesus's meekness. His disciples witnessed it daily. They saw him pray in the Garden of Gethsemane, asking God to spare him from the cross, if it was his will. He cried out, "Father, if thou be willing, remove this cup from me; nevertheless, not my will, but thine be done" (Luke 22:42, KJV). But it was God's will for Jesus to endure the cross. It was part of his plan of salvation for the world, and Jesus submitted to the Father. Jesus was able to look with joy beyond the cross and see all the people who would be saved when they realized what his death on the cross meant for them. (Heb 12:2).

The meekest person I have known in my personal life is my mother, Ruth Lavandie Cason, who has gone on to heaven now. Everyone who knew her would say good things about her. She suffered from extreme poverty, which affected her both mentally and physically. She was deficient in many vitamins and minerals and developed osteoporosis at an early age. The bone degeneration caused her to be bent over from the waist, but she didn't complain. She was full of the Holy Spirit, and she overcame many obstacles in her life. Not only was she an overcomer, but she helped everyone around her. She cared for the sick, and took care of a woman's baby who couldn't do it herself. Even though she had very little, she was always quick to give what she had, and she did it with a willing heart. My mother remained faithful to God all of her days, and her life is an example to me and many others of how to show God's love through humility, meekness, and a willing heart.

I have always wanted to follow my mother's example and bear the fruit of the Spirit in my own life, and I have often prayed and asked God to help me with that. Meekness is probably the one trait of the Holy Spirit I need the most. I have fallen short many times, but there is a scripture I am holding onto. Psalm 138:8 says, "The Lord will perfect that which concerns me: thy mercy, O Lord, endureth forever. Forsake not the work of thine own hands" (NKJV). I trust God, and I believe his word that he is working on my behalf. He cannot fail. Sometimes the circumstance look impossible, but God will do what his word says.

I remember one time when I had just started working at the public library. I had been a stay-at-home mother raising seven children and had not been in the work force for many years. When I first started at the library, everyone was very kind and helpful, and things were going well. Then we got a new librarian. She was totally different from the first one; she seemed moody and was always making changes. At first, I thought she really liked me; she even told me not to worry about my job – that it was secure. Pretty soon, though, she started gossiping about the former librarian and would put her down. I think she began to realize that I really liked the first librarian, and she started to have a different attitude toward me. She started writing me up frequently, and she would show me the letters. It seemed that no matter what I said or did, she would accuse me of either doing something wrong or having wrong motives. I have always felt that I am better at communication when I'm writing rather than speaking, so I would write her a letter and explain my side of things.

One day, three teenage girls from the

county jail came to do community service at the library. The girls were very nice to me and helped me when we re-shelved the books. One of the patrons of the library wrote a letter to the local newspaper stating that the girls from the jail set a bad example for young people and should not be allowed to serve their time there. The letter was printed in the paper and was signed L.M. Even though my initials are M.P., the librarian accused me of writing the letter. I told her that I did not, but she didn't believe me. I went through the library files and found that we had twenty patrons with the initials L.M., but the librarian was convinced I was the one who wrote the letter. It hurt. I felt that she was looking for a reason to fire me and get someone who was more experienced with computers and typing. Righteous indignation welled up inside me, because I knew I was innocent, but God helped me to remain humble, and I remembered the example of Jesus. 1 Peter 2: 18- 23 tells us:

> "Servants, *be* submissive to *your* masters
> with all fear, not only to the good and
> gentle, but also to the harsh. For
> this *is* commendable, if because of
> conscience toward God one endures grief,
> suffering wrongfully. For what credit *is it* if,

when you are beaten for your faults, you take it patiently? But when you do good and suffer, if you take it patiently, this *is* commendable before God. For to this you were called, because Christ also suffered for us, leaving us an example, that you should follow His steps:
"Who committed no sin, Nor was deceit found in His mouth; who, when He was reviled, did not revile in return; when He suffered, He did not threaten, but committed *Himself* to Him who judges righteously..." (NKJV).

I submitted to my boss, and eventually, I did receive a pink slip and was "let go." Everyone missed me at the check-in desk and told me so. A short while later, the librarian who had mistreated me had trouble with the city and wound up having to apologize publicly, on T. V. for something she had said. A long time after that I went back into the library. The librarian seemed happy to see me. I told her the library looked very nice, and she hugged me and said how glad she was to see me. Then she looked at me and said, "Mary, it wasn't worth it." I suppose that was her way of saying she was sorry. I believe she did truly regret the way she treated me. I forgave her, and I hope she's doing well wherever she is.

By keeping a quiet, meek, and humble spirit, I was able to walk in victory even in the midst of this challenging time in my life. I do not have any bitterness toward the woman who wronged me, and I know it was only through the power of the Holy Spirit working in me that I was able to do that. James 3: 13-17 states,

> "Who *is* wise and understanding among you? Let him show by good conduct *that* his works *are done* in the meekness of wisdom. But if you have bitter envy and self-seeking in your hearts, do not boast and lie against the truth. This wisdom does not descend from above, but *is* earthly, sensual, demonic. For where envy and self-seeking *exist,* confusion and every evil thing *are* there. But the wisdom that is from above is first pure, then peaceable, gentle, willing to yield, full of mercy and good fruits, without partiality and without hypocrisy."

When we have the Lord's spirit dwelling in us, we take on his nature, and he gives us the strength to overcome.

I'm sure that every Christian wants to have the fruit of the Spirit at work in their lives.

Jesus teaches that "if we abide in the vine, we will bear much fruit." We abide in him by praying, and reading his word, meditating on it, and keeping our mind on God. Don't become so busy that you forget to pray. The devil is waiting to distract you, so that you will not be prepared to fight the battle. That is why it is so essential that we walk in the Holy Spirit and always have him working through us. Remember that the closer we walk with Jesus, the more of his nature people will see in our lives.

I share this essay with you in closing and hope that something I have said has touched your heart.

One time I went with a women's group to a luncheon in Sulphur Springs, and got to meet the Texas gubernatorial candidate, later to become president, Mr. George W. Bush.

Me (left) with
Dorothy Faye
and Lena May

Epilogue

I finally found the courage to leave Dalton in 1979. One of my daughters was dating a police officer at the time, and she told him all that our family had been through. He lent me money to hire an attorney, and I filed for divorce. The younger kids and I were already living in a separate household from Dalton. When the divorce was final, I was able to pay back the money I had borrowed.

On May 14, 1984, Dalton married Virginia A. Kennedy in Red River County, Texas. Dalton died of a heart attack on January 21, 1992 at the age of seventy-two. We heard reports from two different people that he prayed through before he died. I have forgiven him, and I do not harbor any hard feelings against him. I pray that his soul is at peace.

Afterword
by Rebecca Bolin

Like her mother before her, my mother, Mary Ruth Cason Philips, spent her entire life caring for others. When she was young, she helped her mother care for Icie Faye (her mom's mentally ill sister) and her own sister, Lena May. After marrying and raising seven children, an admirable feat on its own, she went on to raise her granddaughter and two great-grandsons, until they were teenagers. Just when she was about to be free of responsibilities, her oldest daughter, Malinda, was hit by a truck and suffered from a traumatic brain injury. Mother was nearing a point where she needed to be cared for herself, but she would not hear of it. As long as someone needed her, she wanted to be there for them. She took Malinda in and cared for her for the next eight years, with only weekly visits from a home healthcare aide for support. By this time, Mother was in her eighties.

She lived with some of her children over the next few months, until her health deteriorated to the point that she required professional care. She is now a resident at a nursing care facility and is finally able to rest and be cared for. Being free from responsibilities, her personality has begun to flourish. She is learning to express her wishes and take charge of her own life. But more importantly, she is finally free from worry.

The overriding emotion that manifested itself throughout her life was worry. She used to worry herself over everyone and everything: her children, grandchildren, and great grandchildren, people at church, finances, health issues, politics, you name it. She was famous for writing to preachers and asking them to pray for various friends and family members, and she spent quite a bit of time in prayer herself. She had, and still has, a tremendous capacity to believe that God is in control and will move on her behalf if she asks in faith. In addition to her faith, she has peace now. She is relaxed and has a positive outlook. She says she "loves being taken care of."

With the government restrictions on nursing homes during the global pandemic, Mother is unable to have visitors face-to face, but she enjoys talking on the phone and visiting through the glass door. She envisions a bright future for her children, grandchildren, and great grandchildren. She recently recorded a message for them:

"I love you, and I'll be glad when we can have that talk. Y'all all pray for me. If God wants me to be like Sister Allen, [who is currently 102 years old] I know there's, maybe, a couple of things He wants me to do while I'm here...*if* I'm here. If I'm not, then I'll be with Him. So don't y'all be too unhappy. Just be glad that I'm with God and doing His will" (Aug 2020).

(L to R) Dorothy, Robbie Boehler, and me

I am so thankful for my sister, Dorothy Faye (standing). This photo of us was taken on her birthday in 2017.

ABOUT THE AUTHOR

Mary Philips lives in East Texas where she enjoys writing and entertaining family and friends. One of her greatest joys is to sit down with a cup of coffee and laugh and reminisce about old times.

During the global pandemic of 2020, she contracted COVID-19 and was hospitalized. Her condition is stable, now, and she continues to grow stronger each day. She is grateful to all the friends and loved ones who prayed for her.

Made in the USA
Coppell, TX
29 September 2020